By the hard u
to the most beautiful things that have been dragged
out of darkness and into the light.
Everyone is invited to experience the light
of every age and every people.
So, let us walk hand in hand with those from every age.
Let us turn from this brief and transient time
and offer our minds and hearts to the past,
which is long and eternal.

—Seneca, *On the Shortness of Life*

THE CLASSICS CAVE
Sugar Land

THE CLASSICS CAVE

the earliest light for a brighter life

www.theclassicscave.com

THE CLASSICS CAVE is an educational organization centered on the classics of antiquity, with an emphasis on Greece and Rome.

OUR MISSION is to shine the light of the past into the present for a brighter life today.

OUR GOAL is practice—the application of ancient wisdom to our contemporary ways and lives.

WE develop and provide online materials, organize and do outreach, and produce and distribute a variety of print and other media intended to entertain and educate, cultivate and motivate.

VISIT The Classics Cave online (www.theclassicscave.com) to support our mission and to access a growing catalogue of engaging books, useful goods, and other helpful materials for educators and all others interested in benefiting from ancient literature.

IN PRAISE & RECOGNITION OF BASIL THE GREAT

"[*How to Benefit from Reading*] *Greek Literature* is not the anxious admonition of a bigoted ecclesiastic, apprehensive for the supremacy of the Sacred Writings. Rather, it is the educational theory of a cultured man, whose familiarity with classical learning and enthusiasm for it were second only to his knowledge of the Scriptures and zeal for righteousness." —F.M. Padelford, *Essays on Plutarch and Basil*

"We cannot . . . omit consideration of Basil's famous oration on the study of Greek literature and poetry and its value for the education of Christian youth. This document was the charter of all Christian higher education for centuries to come."
—Werner Jaeger, *Early Christianity and Greek Paideia*

"Basil the Great is excellent in all his works. . . . In the arrangement and purity of his ideas he is celebrated as a leader, inferior to no one."
—Photius, Patriarch of Constantinople

"It has then been ordained that the great Basil . . . should now furnish me with the grandest subject that has ever fallen to the lot of an orator. . . . So great a task is the praise of such a man. . . . Come here then and surround me, all you members of his choir, both of the clergy and the laity, both of our own country and from abroad. Aid me in my eulogy. Each of you supply the account of some of his excellences. See him, you occupants of the bench, the lawgiver. See him, you politicians, the statesman. You men of the people, his orderliness. You men of letters, the instructor. . . . You simple men, the guide. . . . The father of orphans, friend of poor men, host of strangers, the man of brotherly love to brothers, the physician of the sick—whatever be their sickness and the healing they need—the preserver of health for the healthy."
—Gregory of Nazianzus, the Theologian
Oration for Basil the Great

"Many bring to the Church of God their profane learning as a kind of gift. Such a man was the great Basil, who acquired the Egyptian wealth [that is, learning from Greek literature] in every respect during his youth and dedicated this wealth to God for the adornment of the Church, the true tabernacle."   —Gregory of Nyssa, *Life of Moses*

"Basil belongs not to the Church of Caesarea alone, nor merely to his own time, nor was he of benefit only to his own kinsmen, but rather to all lands and cities worldwide, and to all people he brought and still brings benefit, and for Christians he always was and will be a most salvific teacher."

—Saint Amphilochius, Bishop of Iconium

"For Basil, to love God meant to love man, whatever man's physical condition or background . . . For [him], doctrine and canon, worship and ethics, word and behavior were inextricably woven."

—Demetrios J. Constantelos
"On Basil the Great's Social Thought and Involvement"

"Basil started out for his life's work with the equipment of the most liberal education which the age could supply. He had studied Greek literature, rhetoric, and philosophy under the most famous teachers. He had been brought into contact with every class of mind. His training had been no narrow hothouse forcing of theological opinion and ecclesiastical sentiment. The world which he was to renounce, to confront, to influence, was not a world unknown to him."

—Blomfield Jackson, "Sketch of the Life and Works of Saint Basil"

"In classical culture, [Basil] yields to none of his contemporaries and is justly placed with the two Gregories among the very first writers among the Greek Fathers. His style is pure, elegant, and vigorous."

—Philip Schaff, *Nicene and Post-Nicene Christianity*

THE BEST OF
BASIL THE GREAT

ON READING LITERATURE
AND EDUCATION

The Best of

Basil the Great

on Reading Literature and Education

The Best Parts in Translation
with
a Narrative Summary of the Rest

including *How to Benefit from Reading Greek Literature*
and Other Selections

selected, introduced, and edited by
The Classics Cave

Cave Best of Series
the best of the classics for today

The Classics Cave
Sugar Land

The Best of Basil the Great on Reading Literature and Education:
The Best Parts in Translation with a Narrative Summary of the Rest

Library of Congress Catalogue-in-Publication Data available on request.

ISBN 978-1-943915-11-8

Published in the United States by
The Classics Cave
P.O. Box 19038
Sugar Land, TX 77496
contact@theclassicscave.com
www.theclassicscave.com

The Classics Cave is an educational organization centered on the classics of antiquity, with an emphasis on Greece and Rome. Our mission is to shine the light of the past into the present for a brighter life today. Our goal is practice—the application of ancient wisdom to our contemporary ways and lives. We develop and provide online materials, organize and do outreach, and produce and distribute a variety of print and other media intended to entertain and educate, cultivate and motivate.

Visit The Classics Cave online (www.theclassicscave.com) to support our mission and to access a growing catalogue of engaging books, useful goods, and other helpful materials for educators and all others who are interested in ancient literature.

For the one entering this great work . . .
Pause for a moment before its door.

Such is the holy gift the Muses give to human beings.
—Hesiod, *Theogony*

CONTENTS

PART 2
Basil and Literature

PART 3
Points of Wisdom & Ways of Practice

OTHER MATTERS OF INTEREST
Related to Basil the Great

The Classics Cave Catalogue

CAVE BEST OF SERIES
INTRODUCTION
The best of the classics for today

H AVE YOU EVER considered how many excellent works of ancient Greek and Latin literature there are to read? Think of all the significant works of poetry and prose—of all the epics, tragedies, comedies, histories, philosophies, orations, biographies, and more!

The problem, of course, is in the approach. How should you read them all? It is The Classics Cave's goal to offer a possible solution— and so the Cave Best of Series, which presents the best of an author, title, or group of authors.

Take the author, title, or group you have in hand. Of the available versions of the work, the Cave Best of Series version is unique for a few reasons. One, it is much shorter than most renditions of the work—oftentimes the number of pages totals anywhere from one-third to one-half of other versions.* Consequently, if you are pressed for time or do not know how many hours you would like to invest in reading the work, then the Cave Best of Series version may be for you.

That is not to say you will not get the whole work—the whole story or discourse or whatever the work centers on. Rather, you will get it in two forms—another unique feature of the Cave Best of Series presentation of a work. Whereas most versions offer either the whole or parts of a work (without any significant explanation of what happens in between each part), the Cave Best of Series version gives you the best or most significant parts in translation, along with a narrative summary of the rest that will tell you exactly what is going on in between. This means you will get the full content, feel, and experience of the work without missing out on anything essential.

And that's important. Unlike study guide versions that offer summary outlines alone, you will have extensive passages and narrative summaries of the whole work that will allow you to judge for yourself what is happening, what characters are central, what themes are significant, what the arguments are and whether they succeed or not, and the like—all depending on the work itself.

This is what the Cave Best of Series offers: the whole work in translated and narrative summary form, making for a relatively quick read that will let you come to terms with the work by yourself.

Not only that but there is also an information-packed introduction that is meant to draw the reader into and answer the most significant questions about the author and the work. Why should we care about *this* author and *this* work? What are the essential facts we should know? What are the work's most important ideas and themes? There is always a full exploration of these points that references the work itself as well as any pertinent scholarship.

Toward the end, there is a section presenting a "Plan of Life" (or something similar), "Points of Wisdom," and "Ways of Practice" related to the author. The latter "Ways" consist of workbook or journal-like prompts and exercises intended to motivate the reader to feel, think, and act in beneficial ways according to the author's "Points of Wisdom."

Finally, there is a unique section called, "Other Matters of Interest Related to [the Author]." It offers additional information about the author, whether a summary of the work, a cast of characters found therein, maps, a glossary of Greek terms, suggestions for further reading, and so on.

In the end, when you read the work as presented in the Cave Best of Series, you will be entertained, educated, and, we at The Classics Cave hope, motivated to practice—to act in an intentional, specific manner toward a better life. With this in mind, welcome to the . . .

Cave Best of Series
the best of the classics for today

---

* Even so, whole, or mostly whole, works are sometimes included in the Cave Best of Series if the work is particularly short.

INTRODUCTION

"Basil belongs not to the Church of Caesarea alone, nor merely to his own time, nor was he of benefit only to his own kinsmen, but rather to all lands and cities worldwide, and to all people he brought and still brings benefit, and for Christians he always was and will be a most salvific teacher."

—Saint Amphilochius, Bishop of Iconium

Have you ever wondered how it is that someone comes to be called "the Great"? Interestingly, we don't encounter any figures with this epithet in philosophy, science, or business. There's no Aristotle the Great, for instance, even though the breadth and depth of his investigations certainly deserve it, if anyone's do. Newton was never called Isaac the Great, nor did anyone ever suggest—to Latinize his name—*Einsteinus Magnus* as another Albert was much earlier called *Albertus Magnus* (Albert the Great). And what about Thomas Edison the Great? Or Henry Ford the Great? Or Steve Jobs the Great? (Imagine the possible title of a biography: *Steve the Great: Computer Mastermind.*) No—not a one has won the title. For examples of people called "the Great," we have to turn back in time and to the realms of politics and religion.

In politics it seems that men who conquer, unify, and rule with great power are counted great. Reaching back to the earliest accounts, there was Cyrus the Great, who conquered much of the ancient Near East, unifying it under the Persian Empire. Later there was Alexander the Great, the Macedonian ruler who conquered the Persian Empire in the name of the Greeks—the same Greeks who had been harassed by the Persians for nearly two hundred years. When the Romans came along and mastered the Greeks, their empire consequently stretched as far as the borders of the old Persian Empire. It was so large, in fact, that in some respects it became unmanageable to govern by one emperor alone. So it was that the emperor Diocletian effectively, if not formally, divided the Roman Empire toward the end of the third century AD. Nevertheless, the emperor Constantine the Great begged to differ with this division. And so, after conquering and winning control of the whole empire, he reestablished unity under his own powerful rule (hence, "the Great").

In the realm of religion, greatness has to do with the scope and subject matter of teaching, as well as personal influence and lifestyle. Take, for example, Anthony the Great, the "Father of Monks." Not only did he sell all and give to the poor, as Jesus advised, but he lived such a radical life that he inspired whole generations of men and women to follow him into the desert in pursuit of a uniquely simple way of life. Scanning over to the other half of the Roman Empire, there was Pope Leo the Great, who was judged so not only for his teaching (he is considered a "Doctor of the Church" by Roman Catholics) but also for his courage in facing Attila the Hun. Leo persuaded the aggressor to leave Italy when he was poised to invade Rome in 452 AD. Finally, Albert the Great—the same *Albertus Magnus* from a moment ago—led a devoutly religious life as a Dominican friar, studying and writing about theology, philosophy, and science. Among other accomplishments, his commentaries on Aristotle and his engagement with Islamic thinkers made him tower above other Medieval scholars.

But why Basil the Great? He was called "Great" very early on by both Gregory of Nyssa and Gregory of Nazianzus. Exploring why he was honored in this way will help us understand why so many over time have cared about this man who lived and taught greatly in the fourth century AD.

WHY SHOULD WE CARE ABOUT BASIL THE GREAT?

The first reason why we should care about Basil is because many others have been intensely interested in and influenced by him over the past nearly two thousand years—many of the highest minds and greatest souls, certainly within the fields of Christian philosophy, theology, and practice. In short, Basil has long been awash with attention and admiration that has, in turn, shaped whole worlds of thought and activity.

Take, for instance, his brother Gregory of Nyssa, who possessed a great philosophical mind in his own right. Introduced to the Greek classics by Basil, Gregory praised him for the immense store of his wealth in learning, what he termed Basil's "Egyptian wealth," and for using it for the benefit of the people of the Church.[1] Without Basil the Great, there would likely have been no Gregory of Nyssa and his more philosophical musings that have also had their own widespread impact.

Although the same may not be said of another Gregory, Basil's dear friend Gregory of Nazianzus (alternatively called Gregory Nazianzen), Basil nevertheless served at times as the great and massive object around which the latter Gregory orbited. In the oration celebrating his friend, Gregory of Nazianzus lauds Basil's high level of education. "What branch of learning did he not traverse?" he asks. "Who had such power in rhetoric . . . in grammar . . . in philosophy?"—as well as astronomy, geometry, and medicine.[2] And yet, whereas Gregory himself admits that he "attained to happiness" in Athens, which had been to him "a city truly of gold and the patroness of all that is good," Basil, though taking full advantage of the opportunities of learning there, judged Athens "an empty happiness."[3] His true pursuit, reports Gregory,

> was philosophy, and breaking away from the world, and fellowship with God—by means of concerning himself amid things below with things above, and winning, where all is unstable and fluctuating, the things that are stable and remain.[4]

It was Basil's influence that ultimately pulled Gregory of Nazianzus away from Athens and in the direction of a different life than he would have otherwise led—an ecclesial and reflective life with its own long-term impact.[5]

In terms of inspiration, and aside from the two Gregories, Basil influenced many Christian thinkers in both the eastern and western Roman Empire. Among them, and somewhat randomly, we may count Ambrose of Milan and Augustine of Hippo in the West, as well as Amphilochius of Iconium and Maximus the Confessor in the East. Centuries later, Thomas Aquinas cited Basil's teaching on "the beginning of time" in creation in his own account of the instantaneous, successionless moment of creation.[6] Even later, when John Calvin attempted to imagine the earliest form of the Church aside from that found in the Acts of the Apostles, it was the "ancient form of the Church" depicted in the writings of "[John] Chrysostom and Basil, among the Greeks" as well as in those of certain Latin fathers that best helped him grasp what it was like.[7]

Though examples may be multiplied, suffice to say that today Basil is considered a "Doctor of the Church" among Roman Catholics, and he carries just as much weight among the eastern Orthodox, where he is counted "a renowned and bright star" and "the revealer of heavenly mysteries."[8] Why? it may be asked. The reasons are many. It is for his defense of Christian orthodoxy against Arianism. It is for his instruction on the Trinity, and, more specifically, on the Holy Spirit in his work *On the Holy Spirit*. It is for his cosmology and his teaching on creation in the *Hexameron*. And this is not to mention the significant contributions he made to the organization of monasticism and to the divine liturgy, his example in serving the poor and the sick, and, finally, the simplicity of his life.

Gregory of Nazianzus compared Basil the Great to the sun beautifully traversing the sky.[9] The image is fitting. Basil shone the light of truth as he understood and experienced it—the truth that he gathered from both Christian and non-Christian sources. It's a point that brings us to the second reason why we should care about Basil, for his role in preserving and promoting non-Christian sources of knowledge and wisdom.

Basil was a man who, in many ways, straddled two worlds. Even though he ended up living much of his life in an atmosphere of Christian feeling, thinking, and acting, he was nevertheless formed by the "pagan" world of Greece and Rome, that which was, as he termed it, "outside" the Church. Basil's education was traditional. It followed the great works of the ancient past going back hundreds of years—as many as a thousand years in the case of Homer and

Hesiod—to the most outstanding writings of the chief thinkers of Greece and Rome: the poets and playwrights, the historians and orators, and, most significantly, the philosophers.

Because he straddled the Christian and the non-Christian worlds in this way, Basil at some point had to rationalize how the two worlds fit together—if at all. I say "if at all" because there was a whole line of Christian thinkers who believed that Christian thinking should have nothing to do with non-Christian thinking— which is to say with Greek and Latin literature, whether in the form of poetry or philosophy. Tertullian was among these.[10] As for the teachings of the Greek philosophers—of those who followed Plato, Aristotle, the Cynics, Epicurus, the Stoics, and others—Tertullian called them "the doctrines of men and of demons produced for itching ears of the spirit of this world's wisdom." Most famously he queried, "What indeed has Athens to do with Jerusalem? What concord is there between the Academy and the Church?"[11] Even so, Tertullian recognized the necessity of "secular studies," of "literary erudition," for the purpose of pursuing "divine studies."[12]

Many other Christian thinkers took a far more positive view. Gregory of Nazianzus, for example, recognized the great advantage of education in "that external culture which many Christians ill-judgingly abhor."[13] Basil agreed—so much so that he wrote a work, the one we have here in hand, explaining how one might benefit from reading Greek literature. Such writings offer a "preliminary training" for the soul. We must, he said, "be initiated into these outside writers if the notion of the good and the beautiful is to remain with us for all time." The point was to learn from "what is useful" in terms of wisdom and the example of a virtuous life.[14]

Writing mid-twentieth century, the scholar of Greek education Werner Jaeger judged that "Basil's famous oration on the study of Greek literature and poetry . . . was the charter of all Christian higher education for centuries to come."[15] This means that Basil's view on the value of non-Christian thinking and literature for Christians became the dominant view as the centuries passed by to the present. So much so, that Pope John XXIII in 1962 declared in his Apostolic Constitution *Veterum Sapientia* (Ancient Wisdom) that

The wisdom of the ancient world, enshrined in Greek and Roman literature, and the truly memorable teaching of ancient peoples, served, surely,
to herald the dawn of the Gospel that God's Son . . . proclaimed on earth.
Such was the view of the Church Fathers and Doctors. In these outstanding literary monuments of antiquity, they recognized man's spiritual
preparation for the supernatural riches that Jesus Christ communicated
to mankind "to give history its fulfillment." Thus the inauguration of
Christianity did not mean the obliteration of man's past achievements.
Nothing was lost that was in any way true, just, noble and beautiful.

Of course, as there is now, there was a third option relative to literature when Basil was alive. If what we may term the "Christian
literature alone" and the "Christian augmented by non-Christian literature" positions were those most often held by Christians, there
were others—including former Christians—who opted for a third
"non-Christian literature alone" position. The most famous of these
was the short-lived Roman emperor Julian. Educated alongside Basil
the Great and Gregory of Nazianzus in Athens, Julian grew up a
Christian, but he later gave up Christianity in order to return to and
gain sustenance alone from the non-Christian traditions of the past.
For this he was later called "the Apostate" (read, *not* "the Great").

Though in different terms, perhaps, the same options relative to
learning and knowledge are available to us today: faith alone, reason
alone, or both; religion alone, science alone, or both. Fortunately, for
those of us who have faith and care to check the "both" box, men
such as Basil the Great led the way in demonstrating how we might
go about reaping a useful, beneficial harvest from what Tertullian
simply and somewhat unhelpfully called "secular learning."

This is the third reason why we should care about Basil the
Great. Not only did he contribute to the preservation of ancient
forms of learning by saying "yes" to non-Christian literature but he
also showed readers *how* to say yes to such a literature—how to
read a literature that was not, strictly speaking, one's own. In this
way, he showed all readers—whether religious or not—how to be
tolerant. We are able to do this, he advised, by highlighting that
which is good, true, and beautiful in a work rather than demanding

a purity of ideology, so to speak, tailor-made for our own way of thinking and our own set of beliefs. This is not to say he tolerated everything in every work. Not at all. In fact, he advised readers not to hand the "rudders of their minds" over to an author indiscriminately. "Instead," he counseled, "you should accept from them only what is useful, and know what to disregard."[16] Still, his general approach, his general assumption, we might say, was positive—the positive expectation to find something worthwhile.

One final point. Although Basil was not the earliest of Christian thinkers and writers, not by nearly three centuries, he nevertheless represents the voice of early Christianity. In common parlance, he is a "Father of the Church," that is, a significant and esteemed teacher from the first seven centuries of the Church's existence. If we wish to understand, therefore, how early Christians thought and approached life, we would do well to listen to Basil. And certainly, if we wish to understand how early Christians interacted with non-Christians and their literature, then Basil is our man.

So, then, who was Basil?

BASIC FACTS ABOUT BASIL THE GREAT

Who was Basil the Great? Basil was a fourth century AD bishop of the Christian Church. He is primarily known for his teaching about the nature of the Holy Spirit, the third person of the Trinity, and for his work in organizing and devising rules for monastic communities. As for the latter, his own work influenced Benedict of Nursia, the chief founder of monasticism in the West.

Born in 329 or 330 AD in Caesarea, in the Roman province of Cappadocia, in what is today central Turkey, Basil grew up in an affluent family of practicing Christians that could trace its Christian lineage back for many generations. He was educated to follow after his father in a career that would have highlighted his talents in rhetoric and the law. Instead, after studying in Caesarea, Constantinople, and Athens, he went on, after a very brief secular career, to devote himself to pursuing and serving God in various ways—as an ascetic monk, a deacon (ordained in 362), a priest (ordained in

365), and, finally, the bishop of Caesarea (ordained in 370). It was during this time, from the 360s through the 370s up to his death in 379 AD, that Basil began to teach and write. Otherwise, he worked to bring aid to the poor and sick, among other activities.

What are Basil's major works? Of his work expounding Christian doctrine and scripture, there are three to note. The *Against Eunomius* defends the orthodox Nicene position of the divinity of Christ (that the Son was God, that is, consubstantial with the Father) against Eunomius and other Arians, who taught that he was a creature and not essentially divine. In this work, Basil cautions the reader to be aware of the human mind's limitations in comprehending and naming the divine reality. The *On the Holy Spirit* defends the proper place of the Holy Spirit as God within the Trinity, and the Holy Spirit's role in the life of individuals and of the Church. Finally, the *Hexameron*, or the *Six Days* (of Creation), offers an exploration of the cosmology or creation account presented in the book of Genesis, emphasizing not only the creation of human beings but their eventual salvation. Aside from these three, Basil additionally prepared countless homilies (we possess many), as well as exegetical reflections on portions of the Bible, such as the Psalms.

Basil also wrote a handful of ascetic writings emphasizing endurance, renunciation, offerings to the poor, and monasticism, among other points having to do with Christian asceticism or practice. Of significance is the *Moralia*, a work that provides eighty rules of life.

He is also known for his many letters, some three hundred, in which he banters with old friends, consoles, offers counsel, and explains Christian teaching and disciplinary practice.

Finally, there is his work offering tips on how his students—how anyone, really—can benefit from reading non-Christian Greek literature. It is to this treatise that we now turn in order to explore some of the more significant themes and ideas he presents therein.

THE BIG THEMES AND IDEAS OF BASIL'S ADDRESS

Listen and receive counsel. In the opening paragraphs of an address intended to advise, Basil directs his students to "eagerly receive my words"—that is, to listen to him and receive his counsel. Why should they do so? To justify himself, Basil turns to Greek literature and, more specifically, to the poet Hesiod.

Before getting on with his explanation, we should note that Basil, with this pivot toward a particular passage of Hesiod and its meaning, is already modeling what he hopes his students will do with Greek literature. They should turn in its direction to understand the nature of the good life and be inspired toward living it. But more on this point as we get to Basil's other ideas and advice.

Returning to the original point, Basil kindly explains that if his students "eagerly receive [his] words," they "will belong to the second category of men praised by Hesiod." What is this category of men like? Quoting the poet, Basil notes that a man in this category is "good and noble" since he is the one "who follows the road mapped out by others."[17]

This description of the good and noble man—the one who listens to and follows advice—comes from Hesiod's *Works and Days*, an epic poem full of epic counsel, in which the poet guides his brother Perses toward "success," ultimately giving him the fundamental ingredients of a happy life.[18] Basil's point, then, is straightforward. The good and noble man follows helpful advice in order to obtain a worthy goal. But more. The goal in this case is not just any random goal; rather, to put it in Aristotle's terms, it is the good that every human being seeks; it is happiness itself, the good life.[19] Implied is the fact that the opposite kind of man does not achieve happiness—the one who doesn't listen to good counsel. Rather, this man—Hesiod calls him "a fool"—ends up with a life of misery and failure.

There's one last point to explore. Young people should not merely follow the counsel of just *anyone*. Rather, they should only be open to the right sort of person. Specifically, this person should be "experienced in human affairs," which means that he or she will likely be older and so will have experienced the "all-instructing vicissitudes of life." Second, it is important that this person cares for the one receiving the advice. Basil, as it happens, is both. "Thanks to my age," he explains, he has been "trained by many experiences." And given his close relationship to his students, he has for them "the same feelings of kindness and goodwill that your own fathers and mothers have."[20]

Read with reserve and discrimination, keeping the goal in mind. Basil fully recognizes what he's up against in advising the young people he is directing. For him, it is a battle of influence. The problem is that every day they go off to school and "encounter the famous thoughts of ancient men through the words they have left behind."[21] Unlike today, perhaps, the very fact that the speakers or writers were ancient was a powerful attraction to people then alive, a fact that meant lineage, heritage, solidity, and, ultimately, truth—at least the atmosphere or appearance thereof. And to add on the fact that the men themselves and their thoughts were famous or notable was to confirm the conclusion drawn from their antiquity. Such men offered up must-know got-to-have-them sayings and thoughts. Who wouldn't want to give him or herself over to them?

Not so fast! Basil cautions. The eager young people in his care should only accept the famous thoughts of old with proper reserve and discrimination. "Here is my advice for you, then," he writes. "You should not once and for all hand over the rudder of your mind to these men—as one might hand over the rudder of a ship to another—to follow along with them wherever they steer you."[22] Later on Basil counsels that "we should not admit everything [we read or hear] without discrimination."[23] The point, again, has to do with the counsel we require to make sure the literature we read—the men and thoughts we give ourselves over to (all those potential captains who wish to take hold of the rudders of our mind)—is such that it will steer us in the right direction.

In the end, the real emphasis is on the latter, the destination, the place where literature may or may not take us. We must judge what we read based on this point. As Basil puts it, "You should accept from them only what is useful."[24] Indeed, he promises that "from this point on . . . I will instruct you in what these useful things are, and how we should go about separating them from the rest."[25]

Returning to the ship and sailing metaphor, Basil points out that "a ship's captain does not randomly deliver his vessel over to the winds without a plan, but he steers the ship directly to port."[26] This means that all readers should have a plan and goal in mind when they read. Realizing that there are all kinds of literature that blow in every direction, we should intentionally, instead of randomly, read. The plan itself should be one that acknowledges the varied nature and direction of literature. Most importantly, our reading should have a goal, some presumably worthwhile port toward which it sails, rather than being aimless.

Value what is truly valuable. In determining what the goal or destination should be, Basil suggests we should understand what is truly valuable or good versus what is not—or what is, we might say, less so. To this end, Basil offers a few general rules by which we may evaluate things.

First, the future life has a value that the present life does not have. "We do not assume, young people, that this human life of ours is altogether something valuable. Nor do we consider or call something entirely good which merely contributes to this life alone."[27] Basil goes on to make the point in this striking manner:

> If someone were to collect every form of prosperity and happiness that has existed from the time when humans first came into being and gather them into a single whole, then he would discover that this collection is not even comparable to the smallest portion of those other goods. On the contrary, all of the goods of this present life together are far removed in worth from the smallest goods of the future life.[28]

Allied to the first rule is another—that we should value soul-matters over body-matters. Basil states that "inasmuch as the soul is more valuable than the body in all things, so great is the difference between the two lives"—that is the future and present lives.[29] In the end, the difference between the future and present and the soul and body is that between reality itself and the "shadows and dreams" we all experience and know that "fall short of reality."[30]

With this latter comparison, Basil points us in the direction of Plato's *Republic* and the famous allegory of the cave.[31] In the allegory, we humans live imprisoned in an unreal world of shadows and echoes that nonetheless seems real. Plato challenges us to break free of our fetters and move out into the light of the sun and the world of real things. As it was for Basil, for Plato the world of real things is that of the soul, which ultimately hungers for and is thus oriented toward the Good itself, that which is true and beautiful.

Take care of your soul—soul care. Given what is truly valuable, Basil counsels that our major concern should be the care of our souls. We should, he says, "devote ourselves to the care of our souls, keeping all our leisure time free from other things."[32]

What is involved in this unique concern? As with any other pursuit, there are dos and don'ts, positives and negatives, things we should cultivate and things we should weed out. We'll focus on the latter in this section and take up the former in the next.

As for the latter, the basic point is that we should not let the body have its way. "We should quiet the restlessness and confusion produced by the body in the soul with the lash of reason."[33] Positively stated, we should work to free our souls from the passions and desires of the body, caring for the body only insofar as it may serve the soul, freeing it to pursue wisdom. "We should not slavishly serve the body any more than is strictly necessary," advises Basil. "Instead, we should provide the soul with the best things. Through the wisdom of philosophy we should free the soul as though from a prison from its association with the passions of the body."[34]

And how may we accomplish this all-important task? We may free our souls by scorning everything that surpasses necessity. Basil defines necessity, or need, in terms of the requirements of nature rather than other perceived needs, including the demands of pleasure—for certain foods, or clothing, or perfumes, or music, or entertainments, or sex and the like. "In all other matters, we must be governed by necessity, only giving to the body as much as is beneficial to the soul."[35]

Let's take a moment away from the major point and look at an aside. In discussing "those who go beyond the bounds of necessity," Basil offers what may be described as an image of addiction, where a person needs more and more in order to satisfy a ravenous urge. Such a person, he says, "resemble[s] people who rush headlong down a slope. They are unable to grab hold of anything to stop their precipitous fall. No, the more they grasp at things, the more things they need to satisfy the desires."[36]

Back to the point. What are some general rules for soul care? Here is the general imperative Basil offers: "Purification of the soul includes scorning those pleasures that satisfy the senses"—those pleasures related to seeing, hearing, smelling, touching, and tasting. Accordingly, we receive the following directives: "We must minister to the belly with what is necessary—but not with pleasant foods, necessarily."[37] And, close "your ears to songs that pour over and utterly destroy your soul. I say this because those passions that are the offspring of cupidity and depravity are naturally produced by this kind of music."[38] And, "I am ashamed to even have to forbid filling the air with whole clouds of sweet smelling perfumes that carry pleasure to your nose, or to smear your body with creams and lotions."[39] And, "what can be said about the importance of not hunting after those pleasures associated with the senses of touch and taste? Such hunting compels those who are devoted to these pleasures to live like wild animals, giving all their attention to the belly and the members below it."[40] Finally, "in a word, every part of the body should be despised by everyone who does not care to be buried in its pleasures as if in filth."[41]

Moving away from the body itself, Basil advises that we should furthermore not pursue wealth or honor. As he puts it, "What use will we have for wealth if we scorn the pleasures that come through the body?"[42] Or, "are we to despise wealth and scorn the pleasures of the senses and yet go on seeking after flattery and adulation . . . ?"[43] Basil has a general rule regarding how best to relate to money: "I believe that we should not yearn after wealth when it is absent. And if it is nearby, we should not make it our purpose to possess it as much as we should to dispose of it well."[44] As for honor, he says, "There is nothing that a prudent man should flee more than living for praise and worrying about what everyone thinks."[45]

Focus on wisdom and the virtues. Whereas the "don't" half of taking care of the soul is aimed at the body, the "do" part centers on the cultivation of wisdom and virtue. The reason for saying "no" to the body is so we may say "yes" to the soul. When we do so—when we, as Plato and Saint Paul say, "make no provision for the body as a location to satisfy the desires" — we create space within ourselves for "the pursuit of wisdom and philosophy."[46] This pursuit, in turn, as if in a feedback loop, is the means by which our souls become freer and freer. "Through the wisdom of philosophy we should free the soul as though from a prison."

More specifically, the means by which we free the soul is virtue (the Greek is *aretē*). Basil tells us that "nearly all those writers who have given us some account of wisdom and philosophy have . . . discoursed in their writings in praise of virtue."[47] This is significant because "it is through virtue that we must enter upon this life of ours," he says.[48] The reason is that virtue is a stable good, the only wealth we may count on that will last forever. "Virtue is the only possession that cannot be taken away. It remains while we are living and when we have completed this life."[49]

It is for this reason that an introduction to the concept and practice of the virtues is absolutely essential for the young. "It is no small advantage," Basil observes, "for a certain friendliness and habitual association with virtue to be produced in the souls of the young."[50] By contrast, "habitual contact with the bad words and deeds of [certain] writings is a road leading to bad behavior."[51] This is so because of the "plasticity of their souls."[52] Given the formable or impressionable nature of a young person's soul or mind, such a one is especially in the position to benefit from literature that declares the value of the good life. To one degree or another, this is true for all of us. Basil accordingly concludes, "if any other man has celebrated virtue . . . , let us favorably receive his words as leading to the same goal as our own."[53] For this reason, Basil turns to the assistance of non-Christian literature, to "outside teachings."

Train with the help of Greek literature. For Basil, this non-Christian literature, including Greek literature, offers a "preliminary training for the eye of the soul."[54] But a preliminary training for what? To explain, Basil uses a number of analogies. "We should see our lives more in terms of athletic contests," he counsels, "or, if you prefer, music competitions. The competitors prepare themselves with practice exercises for the . . . contests in which crowns are offered."[55]

Otherwise we should exercise ourselves as soldiers do in preparation for battle. When we read non-Christian literature, Basil suggests that "we imitate those who perform military drills. They gain experience by means of gymnastic exercises and dances. And when it comes to battle, they benefit from the advantages that come from whatever was done in sport."[56]

The goal of this preliminary training with non-Christian Greek literature, therefore, is twofold. One, it is aimed at a more advanced training in Christian literature, the sacred Scriptures. Two, it is meant to prepare the reader for the contest of life, the stakes of which are "prizes so extraordinary in terms of their extent and sublimity"[57]:

> So then, we must also acknowledge that a contest lies before us—the greatest of all battles for which we must do all things and toil to the best of our abilities until we are prepared. Therefore, we must associate with poets and prose writers and orators and all other men—which is to say with whomever and wherever we may expect to find some benefit relative to the care of our souls.[58]

These are the many non-Christian writers who have written about wisdom and the virtues. And just as certain exercises approximate and so prepare an athlete or soldier for certain athletic contests or battle, so does non-Christian literature prepare a reader for the powerful insights of sacred Scripture and the life that it demands. Basil asserts that such literature is "not entirely different from our own [Christian literature]."[59] As such, it has value.

Yet how can we be certain? As Basil himself seems to pose the question, how can we sufficiently affirm "the fact that knowledge outside of our own is not unprofitable for the soul"?[60]

Moses and Daniel legitimize it. In order to demonstrate that a Christian can benefit from non-Christian literature, that is from a tradition that stands outside the revealed tradition of sacred Scripture (that is, the Old and New Testaments), as well as Church teaching, Basil turns to the examples of Moses and Daniel. As he points out, both men studied non-scriptural wisdom before turning to the divine truth of the sacred Scriptures:

They say, moreover, that even Moses—that most excellent man whose name for wisdom is greatest among all mankind—exercised his mind in the knowledge of the Egyptians, and in this way he approached the contemplation of the one Who Is. They similarly affirm that the wise man Daniel—though in later times—closely examined and thoroughly learned the wisdom of the Chaldeans before partaking in the divine teachings.[61]

How to benefit—read like a bee or a gardener gathering the good and avoiding the bad (examples and warnings). Once Basil establishes the fact that non-Christian literature can be profitable, he turns to how we "should engage with that learning."[62] First, he reminds us to read in a guarded manner, calling to mind his earlier advice to "accept . . . only what is useful and know what to disregard." His concern, as we've already noted, is the defense of the soul:

> We must watch over our souls with every safeguard, so that we may not unknowingly accept something of the worse kind through the pleasure of the poets' words, like those who ingest poisons sweetened with honey.[63]

Basil's ultimate concern, of course, is not merely the defense of the soul but its positive good, "some benefit."[64] As such, there is both a negative aspect to his advice and one that positively searches for the good. What does this look like in practice?

Basil advises that we should only accept some things in what we read and leave the rest alone. In general, we should learn from and imitate the examples of good men. Just as important, however, is the opposite point that we should avoid imitating the examples of bad men.

The idea is at least as old as the late first century BC Roman historian Livy, who explained that

> What chiefly makes the study of history wholesome and profitable is this, that you behold the lessons of every kind of experience set out as on a conspicuous monument. From these you may choose for yourself and for

your own state what examples to imitate. You may also choose what examples to avoid imitating—what is shameful from beginning to end.[65]

Here's how Basil makes the point:

> As for the literature, then, that contains counsel regarding noble conduct, let us receive it in this manner. And since the outstanding deeds of the men of old have also been preserved for us, either by means of an ongoing oral tradition or safeguarded in the words of the poets and prose writers, then let us not overlook this source in terms of benefit.[66]

Basil goes on to offer the examples of Pericles, Eucleides of Megara, Socrates, and Alexander the Great, and suggests how similar they are to examples found in Christian teachings. His conclusion? "Since these exemplary models are close to the teachings found in our own writings, I declare that it is quite valuable for people your age to imitate them."[67]

Basil earlier expresses the general rule of what to accept and what to leave alone: "We will certainly accept those passages of theirs in which they praise virtue and condemn vice."[68] And speaking of the poets—though the prose writers are no different—he says,

> Since every kind of subject is found in their writings, you should not turn your mind to everything found therein, one after another without exception. Rather, whenever they recount for you the words or deeds of good men, you should be pleased with them and admire them, earnestly trying to imitate such as these. But whenever they go through the words and deeds of wicked men, you should avoid such imitation.[69]

Basil offers two images for how we should approach the vast field of non-Christian literature—the images of the bee and the gardener. Here's what he has to say about how the bee gathers the good from a field of flowers:

> Just as bees know how to extract honey from flowers, which to men are enjoyable only for their sweet fragrance and color, even so with literature,

those who look beyond the sweet and agreeable aspects of such writings may gather from them some benefit for their souls. So then, we should engage with literature in a way that follows this image of the bees. For bees neither approach nor land upon every flower without discrimination. Nor do they attempt to carry off the whole flower. Instead, taking only as much as is useful for their work, they are glad to give up the rest. Consequently, if we are wise and moderate, we will acquire from their literature whatever is suitable to us and akin to the truth, while passing over the rest.[70]

He makes the same point with the image of the gardener:

Just as we avoid the thorns while picking flowers from a rose garden, let us guard against what is harmful when gathering whatever is useful from writings such as these.[71]

One last point. Basil presents one other way in which we may benefit by reading non-Christian literature. Not only may we collect what is beneficial but familiarity with the not-so-good or the bad will serve to highlight the tremendous value of the good. To use his analogy of the gardener in the rose garden, it is by seeing the ugliness of the thorns and feeling their pointy prick that we know the beauty and softness of the rose. Placing the two realities side by side, we can appreciate even more the value of the one over the other. Therefore, as Basil observes, "putting ['our own and the other writings'] next to each other, side by side, we can examine the differences between them—which is itself no small advance in establishing the superiority of the better."[72]

Harmonizing your saying and doing—the importance of integrity. The last of Basil's major ideas is one that is fairly straightforward, one that Greeks and Romans had been making for hundreds of years. It is not enough to read or think about the examples of good men. Rather, as Basil advises us, "we must obey these men and attempt to exhibit their words in our lives." His point is that there must be "a correspondence between one's words and deeds"[73]— which is to say that our lives must exhibit integrity if reading good literature is to have any final value for us. We should seek the reality of being good rather than the mere appearance. As such, our reading should motivate our living and doing; to some extent, though it is not merely a functional exercise, we read in order to be and to act. If the latter is not present, then there is something out of line.[74]

In order to illustrate the point, Basil offers several examples. "A musician would not readily play a lyre that is out of tune," he says. "Nor would a chorus leader have a choir that sings together without very much harmony." He finishes with the challenge, "What? Should each man form factions and war within himself? Should his life not agree with his words?"[75]

One last question—that of timing. When should we strive for integrity? Basil admonishes that, given the uncertainty of the future, the time to act is now. "For it would be shameful," he declares, "to squander this present season only to beg for it later on while in distress, when there will be no more time."[76]

LET'S GO!

As we have noted, Basil's advice on how to benefit from reading Greek literature is ultimately aimed at soul care, the care of that deepest, most profound reality in us, and how we might live a life of excellence, of virtue. Unlike the emphasis we find today on "vocabulary acquisition" or "reading comprehension" or "cultural literacy" and the like—all doubtlessly useful things to stress in education and a program of reading—Basil speaks of reading as if the act itself truly matters, as if in reading we do something so serious that it may be likened to preparing for the Olympic games, or, even more serious, for a war in which our future hangs in the balance.

And it *does* matter. For Basil, if we read well, we will likely do well. Let's end, then, with Basil's Pythagorean-inspired encouragement toward the good life:

Let us not shrink from this task because it is difficult and onerous. Rather, let us remember the words of the man who urged everyone to choose the life that is in itself best, in the expectation that this life will become agreeable when we make a habit of it. Accordingly, let us try for the best things.[77]

The "task" Basil refers to is the acquisition of what he terms "traveling supplies," literally the goods that will help us on our way toward a better life.[78]
The Classics Cave invites you to crack open a book with the advice of Basil the Great in mind. Or flip through a magazine. Or enjoy a poem. Whatever you do and whatever you read, Basil would have you do the following: Read with discrimination. Read with purpose. Read to nourish your soul in order to act and be well. If you do, you may find reading taking on a new meaning in your life—beyond utility and entertainment.

NOTES

[1] See Gregory of Nyssa, *The Life of Moses*, trans. by Everett Ferguson and Abraham J. Malherbe (New York: Paulist Press, 1978), 4; 81.
[2] Gregory of Nazianzus, *On Basil the Great, Oration* 43.23.
[3] Ibid., 43.14; 18.
[4] Ibid., 43.13.
[5] See Ibid., 43.24 where Gregory reports that his "longing desire" for Basil caused him to leave Athens (after Basil had already left) and "rush to my mate."
[6] See Saint Thomas Aquinas, *Summa Contra Gentiles, Book Two: Creation*, trans. by James F. Anderson (Notre Dame: University of Notre Dame Press, 1975), 56-58.
[7] See John Dillenberger, ed. *John Calvin: Selections from His Writings* (Atlanta: Scholars Press, 1975), 92.
[8] See "St. Basil the Great, Archbishop of Caesarea in Cappadocia" (www.oca.org).
[9] See the implicit comparisons in Gregory of Nazianzus, *On Basil the Great, Oration* 43.2 and 66.
[10] To one degree or another, others included Saint Paul, Theophilus of Antioch, Justin Martyr, and Jerome. Gregory of Nazianzus recognized there were "many" such Christians. See Gregory of Nazianzus, *On Basil the Great, Oration* 43.11.
[11] Tertullian, *Prescription against the Heretics* 7.
[12] Tertullian, *Of Idolatry* 10.

13 Gregory of Nazianzus, *On Basil the Great, Oration* 43.11.

14 See Basil, *How to Benefit from Reading Greek Literature* 1.5; 2.6-7.

15 Werner Jaeger, *Early Christianity and Greek Paideia* (Cambridge: Harvard University Press, 1961), 81.

16 Basil, *How to Benefit from Reading Greek Literature* 1.5.

17 Ibid., 1.3. We should note that the first category of man is the one "who sees for himself what must be done" — thus, Basil is not merely promoting an authority-based education. And yet, aside from looking into things for oneself, one should pay attention to the counsel of others. For the original passage, see Hesiod, *Works and Days* 293-297.

18 For Hesiod's work, see *The Best of Hesiod's* Theogony & Works and Days (Sugar Land: The Classics Cave, 2020).

19 For more on Aristotle's conception of this good and happiness, as well as the development of the Greek conception of happiness over time from Homer to Plotinus, see *Happiness: What the Ancient Greeks Thought and Said about Happiness* (Sugar Land: The Classics Cave, 2020).

20 See Basil, *How to Benefit from Reading Greek Literature* 1.1-3.

21 Ibid., 1.4.

22 Ibid., 1.5.

23 Ibid., 8.1.

24 Ibid., 1.5. For a similar point, see also 8.1: "We should only accept what is useful." It is important to point out that Basil is not making a utilitarian argument for education. By usefulness he does not mean certain skills (such as critical thinking) or content (such as vocabulary or the content necessary for what E.D. Hirsch calls "cultural literacy"). By usefulness, he very specifically means that which will help one to live a better life.

25 Ibid., 1.5.

26 Ibid., 8.2. In the same section, Basil also uses the images of an archer shooting for a target and a craftsman acting for an end.

27 Ibid., 2.1.

28 Ibid., 2.4.

29 Ibid., 2.5.

30 Ibid., 2.4.

31 See Plato, *Republic* 7.514a-517b.

32 Basil, *How to Benefit from Reading Greek Literature* 9.1.

33 Ibid., 9.15. The reference is to Plato's *Phaedrus* 253c-e, where the charioteer of the soul (the intellect or reason) must control one of the soul's horses — the bad one — by means of "whip and goad."

34 Ibid., 9.2. The background of Basil's idea is once again (in part, at least) Plato. See Plato's *Phaedo* 82e-83a; 64b-c.

[35] Ibid., 9.5. For Basil's definition of need, see 9.18: "And doubtlessly he will define 'need' itself in terms of the necessary requirements of nature, and not in terms of pleasure."

[36] Ibid., 9.19.

[37] Ibid., 9.2.

[38] Ibid., 9.7-8. With this, Basil follows a long line of philosophers beginning with Plato that criticized certain kinds of music and the lyric content of that music as being unhealthy for the soul and for a good life. He states that worthless music was popular in his day (see 9.11). Positively, Basil advises, "We must pursue the other kind of music, which is better in itself and leads to better things" (see 9.8-10). What would he have to say about the sort of music we listen to today? For a fairly recent treatment of the influence music has on the soul, see Allan Bloom, *The Closing of the American Mind* (New York, Simon & Schuster, 1987), 68-81.

[39] Ibid., 9.11.

[40] Ibid., 9.11.

[41] Ibid., 9.12.

[42] Ibid., 9.17.

[43] Ibid., 9.24.

[44] Ibid., 9.21. For a similar early view on the use of wealth, see Clement of Alexandria's *The Rich Man's Salvation*.

[45] Ibid., 9.25.

[46] Ibid., 9.12. The passage from Saint Paul is Romans 13.14: "Put on the Lord Jesus Christ, and make no provision for the flesh, to gratify its desires." For Plato, see *Republic* 6.498b-c.

[47] Basil, *How to Benefit from Reading Greek Literature* 6.1. For a comprehensive presentation of how the ancient Greeks spoke about and understood virtue (or excellence) from Homer to Plotinus, see *Aretē (Excellence or Virtue): What the Ancient Greeks Thought and Said about Aretē* (Sugar Land: The Classics Cave, 2020).

[48] Ibid., 5.1.

[49] Ibid., 5.9.

[50] Ibid., 5.2.

[51] Ibid., 4.2.

[52] Ibid., 5.2.

[53] Ibid., 5.5.

[54] Ibid., 2.6.

[55] Ibid., 8.4.

[56] Ibid., 2.6.

[57] Ibid., 8.10.

[58] Ibid., 2.7.

59 Ibid., 2.6.

60 Ibid., 4.1.

61 Ibid., 3.3-4. See Acts 7.22 and Daniel 1.4.

62 Ibid., 4.1.

63 Ibid., 4.3.

64 Ibid., 2.7.

65 Titus Livius (Livy), *The History of Rome* 1.10. For similar points of view, see also Polybius, *Histories* 1.2, and Diodorus Siculus, *Library* 10.12.1-2 and 15.11.

66 Basil, *How to Benefit from Reading Greek Literature* 7.1.

67 Ibid., 7.7.

68 Ibid., 4.7.

69 Ibid., 4.1-2.

70 Ibid., 4.7-8.

71 Ibid., 4.9.

72 Ibid., 3.1.

73 Ibid., 6.1-2.

74 As Basil puts it, "From the beginning, we should examine at once each one of the teachings and harmonize them with the present goal—according to the Doric proverb, 'Bringing the stone to the line'" (ibid., 4.10).

75 Ibid., 6.4.

76 Ibid., 10.6.

77 Ibid., 10.5. The "words of the man" come from Pythagoras or the Pythagoreans, as noted by Plutarch: "That good precept of the Pythagoreans, 'Make choice of the best life you can, and custom will make it pleasant,' is here also wise and useful" (*On Exile* 8).

78 For Basil's discussion of traveling supplies, see Basil, *How to Benefit from Reading Greek Literature* 10.3-5.

PART 1

How to Benefit from Reading Greek Literature

— An Address to Students —

Basil the Great

THE GOAL

HOW TO BENEFIT FROM ANCIENT LITERATURE

IN BRIEF: *Given his life experience and his warm relationship with his students, Basil declares his wish to offer them direction in life by showing them how to benefit from reading ancient literature. His intention is to explain how they may maintain control of their own minds while determining what is useful and what is not.*

THERE ARE MANY considerations that summon me to advise you, young people, on what I judge to be the most excellent things—those things which I am sure will benefit you if you accept them. First, I am able to map out the safest road for those who are just beginning the journey of life. Thanks to my own age, I am in the position to do this since I have already been trained by many experiences and have participated well enough in the all-instructing vicissitudes of life, both good and bad.[1] Consequently, I am experienced in human affairs. [2] Second, inasmuch as I come directly after your parents in natural relationship to you, I myself have for you the same feelings of kindness and goodwill that your own fathers and mothers have. And unless I am utterly wrong in my reading of you, I believe that you do not yearn for your parents when you are with me.

[3] So then, if you eagerly receive my words, you will belong to the second category of men praised by Hesiod. And if you do not—well, I should say nothing unfriendly—so remember for yourselves the passage in which he says, "The best man is the one who sees for himself what must be done. The one who follows the road mapped out by others is also good and noble. But the one who does neither is useless in everything he does."[2]

[4] Do not be surprised, then, if I say that I have discovered something profitable for you who go to school every day and encounter the famous thoughts of ancient men through the words they have left behind. [5] Here is my advice for you, then: you should not once and for all hand over the rudder of your mind to these men—as one might hand over the rudder of a ship to another—to follow along with them wherever they steer you.[3] Instead, you should accept from them only what is useful and know what to disregard.

From this point on, therefore, I will instruct you in what these useful things are, and how we should go about separating them from the rest.

NOTES

[1] Compare with what the historian Polybius has to say regarding the study of history and the recollection of the "catastrophes of others"—it is "the only method of learning how to bear with dignity the vicissitudes of fortune" (*Histories* 1.1.2).

[2] Hesiod, *Works and Days* 293-297.

[3] The notion of handing over the rudder of the mind to others appears in *Clitophon* 408b, a dialogue attributed to Plato but not likely by him.

This Life and the Next
What Is and Is Not Valuable, and How to Train

IN BRIEF: *Basil describes the great difference in value between this present life and the future life, one that is similar to the vast difference between shadows and real things. Consequently, his students must be oriented to and prepare themselves for the life to come. The sacred writings found in the Bible are the primary means by which they may do so. Nevertheless, for people who are too young to dive into the profound teachings of these writings—as Basil's students are, he contends—it is beneficial to prepare by other means, namely, by means of literature outside the sacred writings. Paying attention to the good found in this other literature, his students will then be able to turn to the sacred writings once they are older and ready.*

W E DO NOT assume, young people, that this human life of ours is altogether something valuable. Nor do we consider or call something entirely good which merely contributes to this life alone. [2] Accordingly, we judge neither well-known ancestors, nor bodily strength, nor beauty, nor stature, nor honors given by all humankind, nor kingship itself, nor anything else we men call great, worthy of our aspirations or prayers.[1] Nor do we gaze upon the owners of these things with admiration. Rather, with hope we move on toward a distant time, and everything we do is a preparation for the other life. [3] Consequently, we declare that we must love whatever contributes to that life and pursue it with all our strength. On the other hand, we must disregard as worthless whatever does not accomplish this end.

Now, given our present purpose, it would take too long to discuss what this life will be like, and how and in what manner we will live it. Not only that, but such a discussion is for the more mature to listen to than for hearers your age.

[4] And yet, after saying this much, I may perhaps be able to point out to you that if someone were to collect every form of prosperity and happiness that has existed from the time when humans first came into being and gather them into a single whole, then he would discover that this collection is not even comparable to the smallest portion of those other goods. On the contrary, all of the goods of this present life together are far removed in worth from the smallest goods of the future life, even as shadows and dreams fall short of reality.[2] [5] Or, to offer an example that is much closer to home, inasmuch as the soul is more valuable than the body in all things, so great is the difference between the two lives.

Now, our sacred writings lead us toward this future life by teaching us ineffable mysteries. [6] That said, as long as you are young and you are therefore unable to understand the profound meaning of these writings, we offer by means of shadows and reflections, so to speak, a preliminary training for the eye of the soul by means of other writings that are not entirely different from our own.[3] In this way, we imitate those who perform military drills. They gain experience by means of gymnastic exercises and dances. And when it comes to battle, they benefit from the advantages that come from whatever was done in sport.

[7] So then, we must also acknowledge that a contest lies before us—the greatest of all battles for which we must do all things and toil to the best of our abilities until we are prepared.[4] Therefore, we must associate with poets and prose writers and orators and all other men—which is to say with whomever and wherever we may expect to find some benefit relative to the care of our souls. [8] Just as dyers prepare the cloth before they apply the dye—whether it is purple or any other color—so must we also be initiated into these outside writers if the notion of the good and the beautiful is to remain with us for all time.[5] Then, once we are ready, we will listen to the ineffable mysteries taught in the sacred writings. And like those who have become accustomed to seeing the reflection of the sun in the water, we will then direct our eyes to the light.[6]

NOTES

[1] For a similar list, see Plato, *Republic* 4.491.

[2] Compare the notion of "shadows and dreams fall[ing] short of reality" to Plato's allegory of the cave in the *Republic* 7.514a-517b.

[3] N.G. Wilson explains that "preliminary training (*progumnazometha*)" was the "technical term used among ancient educational theorists" for initial training and learning. See N.G. Wilson, *Saint Basil on Greek Literature* (London: Gerald Duckworth & Co., 1975), 43. For a general exposition of this training, see Raffaella Cribiore, *Gymnastics of the Mind: Greek Education in Hellenistic and Roman Egypt* (Princeton: Princeton University Press, 2001). For "eye of the soul," see Plato, *Republic* 7.533d.

[4] Compare to 1 Corinthians 9.24-25 and Hebrews 12.1, as well as Plato, *Republic* 10.608b.

[5] For a similar analogy referring to dyers, see Plato, *Republic* 4.429d-e.

[6] For some idea of the "ineffable mysteries" in the Greek tradition, see Plato's *Symposium* 209e-210b. For directing one's eyes to the light after getting used to "seeing the reflection of the sun in the water," see Plato, *Republic* 7.516a-b, as well as Plutarch, *How Adolescents Should Study Poetry* 36e.

CHRISTIAN AND NON-CHRISTIAN WRITINGS
LIKE A TREE, ITS FRUIT AND LEAVES

IN BRIEF: *Basil explores how Christian and non-Christian writings corre-spond to each other and what the role of each is in education. He settles upon the image of a tree with its fruit and leaves. Although the fruit is the proper excellence of a tree, the leaves nonetheless serve it in their own way and excellence. Similarly, both Christian truth and non-Christian wisdom are proper to and useful for the soul. Basil offers the biblical Moses and Daniel as examples. Both men studied non-scriptural wisdom before turn-ing to the divine truth of the sacred Scriptures.*

S O THEN, IF there is some affinity between our own and the other writings, then knowledge of them should be useful to us. If not, at least by putting them next to each other, side by side, we can examine the differences between them—which is itself no small ad-vance in establishing the superiority of the better.

[2] With what may we now liken the two sorts of education in order to obtain an image or simile? Perhaps something like this. Just as it is the proper virtue of a tree to abound with beautiful fruit produced during the right season, but at the same time the tree also grows deco-rative leaves that wave and dance around its branches, even so, with the soul, truth is its real and primary fruit, yet it is not objectionable for the soul to be surrounded by outside wisdom, even as a tree's leaves provide shelter for its fruit and a flourishing appearance.

[3] They say, moreover, that even Moses—that most excellent man whose name for wisdom is greatest among all mankind—ex-ercised his mind in the knowledge of the Egyptians, and in this way he approached the contemplation of the one Who Is.[1] [4] They sim-ilarly affirm that the wise man Daniel—though in later times—

closely examined and thoroughly learned the wisdom of the Chaldeans before partaking in the divine teachings.[2]

NOTES

[1] For Moses' education and the notion of God as "I Am," see Acts 7.22 and Exodus 3.14.

[2] For Daniel's education, see Daniel 1.4-5.

HOW TO ENGAGE WITH LITERATURE
SEEKING WHAT IS USEFUL, LIKE A BEE OR GARDENER

IN BRIEF: *Basil discusses how one may benefit from non-Christian litera-ture. Whether reading poetry or prose, the key is to focus on that which praises virtue and to avoid that which glorifies vice. A reader may do this by imitating the bee, which gathers what is useful from the flower while leaving alone what is merely pleasurable. One may also imitate a gardener, who successfully gathers roses while avoiding their thorns.*

WELL, THE FACT that knowledge outside of our own is not un-profitable for the soul has been sufficiently affirmed. The next point I will discuss, then, is just how you should engage with that learning.

First, I should begin with the writings that come from the poets. Since every kind of subject is found in their writings, you should not turn your mind to everything found therein, one after another without exception. Rather, whenever they recount for you the words or deeds of good men, you should be pleased with them and admire them, earnestly trying to imitate such as these. [2] But when-ever they go through the words and deeds of wicked men, you should avoid such imitation, stopping up your ears just as much as Odysseus did, as the poets affirm, when he avoided the songs of the Sirens.[1] I say this because habitual contact with the bad words and deeds of these writings is a road leading to bad behavior.

[3] Therefore, we must watch over our souls with every safe-guard, so that we may not unknowingly accept something of the worse kind through the pleasure of the poets' words, like those who ingest poisons sweetened with honey.[2] [4] We will not, therefore, praise the poets when they abuse or scoff at others. Nor when they

portray people engaged in passionate love affairs or drinking to the point of intoxication.[3] Nor when they define happiness in terms of tables brimming with food and depraved songs.[4] We will least of all pay attention to them when they tell stories or say anything about the gods—especially when they go on about the plural number of the gods and about the lack of harmony among them.[5] [5] For in their stories, brothers form factions against brothers, as do parents against children, and, yet again, offspring wage endless war against their parents. As for the gods' adulterous affairs and their passionate desires and their sexual acts done in public—especially those of Zeus, the chief god and highest of all, as the poets themselves say—all things which we cannot mention without blushing, even in connection with cattle and other animals, we will leave all these to stage actors.[6]

[6] I have the same things to say about prose writers—especially whenever they fabricate stories for the amusement of their audience. And certainly we will not imitate the public speakers in their art of lying—the rhetoricians, orators, and politicians. For neither in courts of law nor in other affairs is lying right for us who have chosen the straight and true way of life, and for whom the prosecution of lawsuits is forbidden by law.[7]

[7] Rather, we will certainly accept those passages of theirs in which they praise virtue and condemn vice. For just as bees know how to extract honey from flowers, which to men are enjoyable only for their sweet fragrance and color, even so with literature, those who look beyond the sweet and agreeable aspects of such writings may gather from them some benefit for their souls.[8]

[8] So then, we should engage with literature in a way that follows this image of the bees. For bees neither approach nor land upon every flower without discrimination. Nor do they attempt to carry off the whole flower. Instead, taking only as much as is useful for their work, they are glad to give up the rest. [9] Consequently, if we are wise and moderate, we will acquire from their literature whatever is suitable to us and akin to the truth, while passing over the rest. And just as we avoid the thorns while picking flowers from a rose garden, let us guard against what is harmful when gathering

whatever is useful from writings such as these.⁹ [10] Therefore, from the beginning, we should examine at once each one of the teachings and harmonize them with the present goal—according to the Doric proverb, "Bringing the stone to the line."¹⁰

Notes

¹ See Homer, *Odyssey* 12.39-54 and 165-200, as well as Basil, *Letter* 1. Interestingly, Basil seems to get the details wrong in referring to this episode. He suggests that Odysseus himself stopped up his ears with wax, when, according to the *Odyssey*, it was only his comrades who did so, while he, tied to the ship's mast, listened to the Sirens. Even so, it was Odysseus who made the provision for the wax and ordered his men to tie him to the mast so he would not experience harm in listening to their beautiful voices.

² The notion of watching over or guarding one's soul or heart is present in Proverbs 4.16: "Above all else, guard your heart, for everything you do flows from it."

³ Basil may have the poetry of Anacreon (sixth century BC) and the Anacreon-inspired *Anacreontea* in mind—poetry that glorifies wine and love-making. That suggested, the possibilities are too many to identify his source with any precision.

⁴ See, for example, Homer, *Odyssey* 9.5-11 and Odysseus' declaration to the Phaeacian king Alcinous: "As for me, I declare that there is nothing better or more delightful than when a whole people join in merry festivity together, with the guests sitting side by side listening to the singer, while before them the table is loaded with bread and meats, and the cupbearer draws wine from the mixing bowl and pours it into all the goblets. In my mind, this seems to be the most beautiful thing."

⁵ His refusal to "pay attention" is doubtlessly inspired by Socrates in Plato's *Republic* Books 2 and 3.

⁶ Among other sources, we find such stories in Homer's *Iliad* and *Odyssey*, as well as in Hesiod's *Theogony*. Basil may have in mind the Trojan War, in which the gods formed factions against one another, or the great Titanomachy (the Titan-battle) related in Hesiod's *Theogony*, in which the younger generation of Olympian gods waged war against the older generation of Titans, who, led by Kronos, had themselves ambushed their own progenitor (Ouranos), cutting off his genitals. As for love-making, he may have in mind Zeus' outdoor encounter with Hera (*Iliad* 14) or Ares' passionate affair with Aphrodite (*Odyssey* 8). Whatever Basil precisely had in mind, the embarrassment, outrage, or just plain puzzlement caused by these and many other passages had existed for

centuries. N.G. Wilson informs us that "embarrassing passages of Homer had led to the development of allegorical interpretations as early as Theagenes of Rhegion (c. 525 BC)" (*Saint Basil on Greek Literature*, 47).

[7] See 1 Corinthians 6.1-7.

[8] Compare what the Athenian orator Isocrates (436-338 BC) says to Demonicus: "For just as we see the bee settling on all the flowers and sipping the best from each, so also those who strive for education and culture should not leave anything untasted, but they should collect useful knowledge from every source" (*To Demonicus* 1.52). For a similar image, see Plutarch, *How a Man May Become Aware of His Progress in Virtue* 8 (*Moralia* 79c-d).

[9] F.M. Padelford rightly explains that "the general attitude taken here toward selectiveness in reading is Platonic." He cites both Plato's *Republic* and *Laws* to make the point. See Frederick Morgan Padelford, *Essays on the Study and Use of Poetry by Plutarch and Basil the Great* (New York: Henry Hold and Company, 1902), 105.

[10] The proverb was apparently popular during this time (the fourth and fifth centuries AD)—both Gregory of Nazianzus and John Chrysostom cite it in their own work. N.G. Wilson notes, "While [the proverb] is cited by the fathers, I have not found any use of it in a classical author that is likely to have served as Basil's source" (*Saint Basil on Greek Literature*, 50).

POETRY

PAYING ATTENTION TO VIRTUE IN POETRY

IN BRIEF: *Basil advises the young to pay attention to those passages in poetry and other writing having to do with virtue. Given the responsive and formable nature of their minds, this point is particularly important for them. He goes on to mention and give examples from five Greek authors (Hesiod, Homer, Solon, Theognis, Prodicus), who praise virtue and call on men to travel along her road rather than that of vice. All stress the superiority and benefits of virtue as compared with vice, as well as any other object or experience typically valued by humans.*

SINCE IT IS through virtue that we must enter upon this life of ours, and since much has been said in celebration of virtue by the poets and prose writers, and even more by the philosophers, we must particularly turn our attention and apply ourselves to such literature.[1] [2] I say all this because it is no small advantage for a certain friendliness and habitual association with virtue to be produced in the souls of the young. This is so because the learning of the young is most likely indelible since it has been deeply stamped upon them by reason of the plasticity of their souls.[2]

[3] Or what else, if not an exhortation for the young to virtue, are we to assume Hesiod had in mind when he composed the following verses that everyone is singing? That—"the steep road that leads to virtue is at first rugged and hard to travel, full of much sweat and lengthy toil."[3]

[4] Therefore, it is not for everyone to advance along this uphill road, nor, once advancing, is it easy to reach the summit. Still, when a man has reached the top, he sees that the road is smooth and beautiful and easy to travel over. It is more pleasant than the other road

that leads to wickedness—which one may have in abundance from near at hand, as the same poet says. [5] It seems to me that Hesiod had no other purpose in making these points than to turn us toward virtue and summon all men to be good, and so that we might not become weak and cowardly when faced with suffering and toil, quitting before we reach the goal.

And, to be sure, if any other man has celebrated virtue in the manner of Hesiod, let us favorably receive his words as leading to the same goal as our own.

[6] Now, as I myself have heard a man say who is skillful at closely examining the mind and meaning of a poet, all Homer's poetry is a commendation of virtue.[4] And with Homer, everything apart from what is incidental leads to this end—not least of which are those lines where he makes the princess stand in awe of the leader of the Cephallenians when Odysseus first appears alone and naked after being saved from the shipwreck. Even so, since Homer portrays him as adorned with virtue instead of clothing, he was far from incurring shame by merely being seen naked. [7] Thereafter, indeed, the rest of the Phaeacians counted him worthy of reverence, handing over to him the luxury by which they lived. They all looked on him with admiration, counting him fortunate. And there was not one Phaeacian at that moment who longed for anything else but to become Odysseus—the same one just saved from the shipwreck.[5] [8] The interpreter of the poet's meaning said that Homer practically shouts it aloud in these passages, saying, "You must care for virtue, men—virtue, which swims ashore with the shipwrecked man and makes him, when he comes naked to dry land, more honored than the prosperous Phaeacians."

[9] And indeed, such is the case. As in a game of dice, all other possessions belong to the possessor no more than to any other man who chances to win, shifting from this one to the other. Virtue is the only possession that cannot be taken away.[6] It remains while we are living and when we have completed this life. As it seems to me, it was for this reason, indeed, that Solon said the following while addressing the wealthy: "But we will not exchange with them our virtue for their wealth since the one lasts forever, while money and

possessions change their owners from day to day."

[10] Nearly resembling these sentiments are those words from Theognis in which he declares that the god—whatever he may mean by saying "the god"—inclines the scale for men at one time *this* way and at another time *that* way, now to be wealthy but now to have nothing.

[11] Furthermore, Prodicus, the sophist from Ceos, explored similar notions regarding virtue and vice in his own writings. Therefore, we must also apply our minds to him, not tossing the man out as worthless. [12] Prodicus' account goes something like the following—as far as I can recall the man's thoughts, anyway. I do not know the account word for word, but only that he spoke without meter in this way: When Heracles was quite young, just about your age right now, he was considering which road he should take—the one leading through suffering and toil to virtue or the easiest road. Just then, two women approached. These were Virtue and Vice.

[13] Now, even though they were silent, the difference between them was evident in their appearance. The one woman had been decked out for beauty through the art of embellishment. She was overflowing with extravagance, taking with her every stream of pleasure dependent on vice. Now, with these things displayed, and promising even more than these, she endeavored to drag Heracles to her. [14] But the other woman was lean and unwashed. She looked at him intensely, speaking differently to him. For she promised nothing relaxed or pleasant. Instead, she offered him a whole ocean of sweat—countless sufferings and toils and dangers through every land and sea. Nevertheless, the prize for these was to become a god—or so Prodicus' account has it. In the end, Heracles followed the latter woman.[7]

NOTES

[1] For a comprehensive presentation of how the ancient Greeks spoke about and understood virtue (or excellence) from Homer to Plotinus, see *Aretē (Excellence*

or Virtue): What the Ancient Greeks Thought and Said about Aretē (Sugar Land: The Classics Cave, 2020).

[2] Compare to Seneca, *Letter* 108.12: ". . . When the mind is young, it may most easily be won over to desire what is honorable and upright." And Plutarch, *On the Education of Children* 5 (*Moralia* 3e-f): "For childhood is a tender thing and easily wrought into any shape. The souls of children readily receive the impressions of those things that are dropped into them while they are yet but soft. . . . And as soft wax is apt to take the stamp of the seal, so are the minds of children to receive the instructions imprinted on them at that age."

[3] See Hesiod, *Works and Days* 289-291. Lilah Grace Canevaro reports that this one passage alone "is quoted some twenty-six times in extant literature dating from 70 BC to AD 300." See Lilah Grace Canevaro, *Hesiod's Works & Days: How to Teach Self-Sufficiency* (Oxford: Oxford University Press, 2015), 8. If we reference earlier Greek literature, the number of citations expands, including writers such as Plato and Xenophon.

[4] N.G. Wilson notes that "this view of Homer's poetry, which helped it to maintain its position in the educational curriculum, is seen in Dio Chrysostom 43 [*sic*], Horace *Epistles* 1.2.1-4, and most fully in the scholia [anonymous commentary] on the *Iliad*. . . . In these scholia the attempt to draw a moral lesson from each episode is taken to great lengths . . ." (*Saint Basil on Greek Literature*, 52). Dio Chrysostom, for instance, states, ". . . It would be a great task if one should recount all that Homer composed about virtue and vice . . ." (*Oration* 53).

[5] See *Odyssey* 6.135-243; 7.142ff.; 8.17-23 and 387-397.

[6] Compare to one of the Cynic Antisthenes' sayings: "Virtue is a weapon that cannot be taken away" (Diogenes Laertius, *Lives and Opinions of Eminent Philosophers* 6.12). For more on the Cynics and Cynic philosophy, see *The Cynics: Cynic Philosophy for Desiring, Enduring & Living Well* (Sugar Land: The Classics Cave, 2020) or *The Best of the Cynics* (Sugar Land: The Classics Cave, 2020).

[7] For another telling of Prodicus' story, see Xenophon, *Memorabilia* 2.1-34.

THE IMPORTANCE OF INTEGRITY
MATCHING WORDS WITH DEEDS

IN BRIEF: *Basil stresses the value of lining up one's actions with what one says and thinks. One should not merely strive for the appearance of virtue but its reality.*

A ND NEARLY ALL those writers who have given us some account of wisdom and philosophy have, to one degree or another and according to the ability of each, discoursed in their writings in praise of virtue.[1]

We must obey these men and attempt to exhibit their words in our lives, just as the man does who firmly establishes his pursuit of wisdom with works, while philosophy is a matter of words for other men. "He alone is wise, whereas the others cast about like shadows."

[2] It seems to me that such a correspondence between one's words and deeds is very much as if a painter of live models had represented a man of quite wondrous beauty, and this same man would in reality be as the painter had displayed him on his panels.[2]

[3] On the other hand, when a man brilliantly praises virtue in public, going on and on about it with long speeches, while in private he values what is pleasant before moderation, and outdoing others before justice, I would say that such a man resembles those stage actors who put on dramas, often appearing on stage as kings and masters even though they are neither kings nor masters, and perhaps not even free men at all. [4] Again, a musician would not readily play a lyre that is out of tune. Nor would a chorus leader have a choir that sings together without very much harmony. What? Should each man form factions and war within himself? Should his life not agree with his words?

[5] Nevertheless, quoting Euripides, one will say, "The tongue has sworn, but the mind is not bound by the oath."[3] Such a man seeks the appearance of being good rather than actually being good. Even so, this is the height of injustice—if we must obey the words of Plato, which forbid the appearance of being just without actually being so.[4]

NOTES

[1] For a comprehensive presentation of how the ancient Greeks spoke about and understood virtue (or excellence) from Homer to Plotinus, see *Aretē (Excellence or Virtue): What the Ancient Greeks Thought and Said about Aretē* (Sugar Land: The Classics Cave, 2020).

[2] Though somewhat different, compare to Basil's *Letter* 2: "Generally, as painters, when they are painting from other pictures, constantly look at the model, and do their best to transfer its lineaments to their own work, so too must he who is desirous of rendering himself perfect in all branches of excellence, keep his eyes turned to the lives of the saints, as though to living and moving statues, and make their virtue his own by imitation."

[3] Euripides, *Hippolytus* 612.

[4] See Plato, *Republic* 2.361a and *Gorgias* 527b.

OUTSTANDING DEEDS
EXEMPLARY MODELS BY WHICH TO LIVE

IN BRIEF: *Basil counsels his students to take into account and imitate the examples of noble conduct and outstanding deeds from the past. These examples may serve as models. Among those on display are Pericles of Athens, Eucleides of Megara, the philosopher Socrates, Alexander the Great, and Cleinias, the disciple of Pythagoras. Basil asserts that these men exemplify a handful of Christian principles: turning the other cheek; enduring another man's anger with patience and wishing for his good; avoiding lust in one's heart; and refusing to swear an oath.*

A S FOR THE literature, then, that contains counsel regarding noble conduct, let us receive it in this manner. And since the outstanding deeds of the men of old have also been preserved for us, either by means of an ongoing oral tradition or safeguarded in the words of the poets and prose writers, then let us not overlook this source in terms of benefit.[1]

[2] For example, a certain man from the market kept railing at Pericles. But the latter paid no attention to him. Still, the man kept it up all day long, mercilessly abusing him. And yet he just went on ignoring it. Then, when it was already evening and dark, Pericles escorted the man home with a light even though the man kept it up. He did this so that his training in philosophy might not be utterly spoiled.[2]

[3] Yet again, a certain man who was provoked to anger by Eucleides of Megara threatened him with death and vowed to kill him. Eucleides, however, took a counter-oath. He swore that he would appease the man and make him put an end to his angry feelings against him.[3]

How valuable it is to have such exemplary models in mind when a man is seized by anger! [4] For one must not simply trust in and rely upon the tragedy when it says, "Against enemies, anger arms the hand."[4] On the contrary, we should desist from anger altogether. If this is not easy to achieve, we should at least employ reason as a kind of bridle so as not to allow anger to carry us beyond what is appropriate.[5]

[5] But let us bring our discussion back again to the exemplary models of outstanding deeds. A certain man kept striking Socrates, the son of Sophroniscus, in the face, attacking him without mercy. Even so, he did not oppose the man. Rather, he allowed the man, who was drunk with wine, to take his fill of anger, so that his face ended up swollen and bruised thanks to the blows. [6] Now, when the man stopped striking him, Socrates, it is said, did nothing more than write on his forehead in the manner of a sculptor signing a sculpture, "So-and-so made this." So far did Socrates defend himself.[6]

[7] Since these exemplary models are close to the teachings found in our own writings, I declare that it is quite valuable for people your age to imitate them. For this example of Socrates is akin to that precept of ours which says that we should not defend ourselves against the man who strikes us on the cheek; rather, we should also offer the other cheek. [8] And the example of Pericles or Eucleides is akin to the precept that we should submit to those who persecute us and gently endure their anger. And this other precept too—that we should pray for our enemies, wishing the good for them instead of cursing them.[7] Whoever has been first instructed with the exemplary models found in these writings will not afterwards distrust those precepts found in our writings as impossible or impracticable.

[9] I should not pass over the example of Alexander, who would not even look at the captured daughters of Darius, who had a reputation for stunning beauty.[8] He judged it shameful for one who had conquered men to be a slave to women. This example accords with our own precept that he who looks at a woman for the sake of pleasure, even though he is not actually committing the act of adultery, is not cleared of every charge since he has received the desire into his soul.[9]

[10] As for the example of Cleinias, one of the disciples of Pythagoras, it is difficult to believe that it is by mere chance that it coincides with the precepts found in our own writings, rather than an intentional imitation of them. What, then, did Cleinias do? Although it was possible to escape a fine of three talents by taking an oath, he paid the fine rather than swearing—even though he could have sworn truthfully.[10] It seems to me that he must have heard the command that bars us from taking an oath.[11]

NOTES

[1] We should note that Basil is not praising the whole life, with its every deed and dimension, of the following examples, but only that which is wise and virtuous.

[2] For the story about Pericles (though slightly different), see Plutarch, *Pericles* 5.

[3] For the account regarding Eucleides the Socratic, see Plutarch, *On the Control of Anger* 14 (*Moralia* 462c) and *On Brotherly Love* 18 (*Moralia* 489d).

[4] The reference appears to be to Euripides, *Rhesus* 84.

[5] For the notion of using reason as a bridle (as a charioteer would rein in a troublesome horse), see Plato, *Phaedrus* 254c-e.

[6] Diogenes Laertius relates similar stories about the Cynics Diogenes of Sinope and Crates of Thebes (*Lives and Opinions of Eminent Philosophers* 6.33 and 6.89).

[7] For the scriptural foundation of the precepts, see Matthew 5.39: "But I tell you, do not resist an evil person. If anyone slaps you on the right cheek, turn to them the other cheek also"; and 5.44: "I tell you, love your enemies and pray for those who persecute you."

[8] For similar accounts, though not identical in details, see Arrian, *Anabasis* 4.19.6 and Plutarch, *Life of Alexander* 21.

[9] See Matthew 5.27-28: "You have heard that it was said, 'You shall not commit adultery.' But I tell you that anyone who looks at a woman lustfully has already committed adultery with her in his heart."

[10] For the story about Cleinias (thought Iamblichus does not mention him by name), see Iamblichus, *Life of Pythagoras* 144.

[11] Matthew 5.34-37: "But I tell you, do not swear an oath at all: either by heaven, for it is God's throne; or by earth, for it is his footstool; or by Jerusalem, for it is the city of the Great King. And do not swear by your head, for you cannot make even one hair white or black. All you need to say is simply 'Yes' or 'No'; anything beyond this comes from the evil one."

KEEPING IN MIND THE FINAL GOAL
TRAIN HARD, TAKING IN WHAT IS USEFUL

IN BRIEF: *Basil returns to his original and primary point—that readers should only take in what is useful from literature rather than everything without discrimination. When reading, readers should always keep in mind the ultimate goal. Among other examples, Basil suggests that readers should behave like a ship's captain guiding his ship into port, or a musician or an athlete preparing for a contest. He mentions the renowned musician Timotheus, and the athletes Polydamas and Milo. As for the latter, in order to take first prize, an athlete keeps his mind on the goal of winning the contest by rigorously training and by enduring many hardships and the harsh advice of his trainers. So too should the young and others attentively and actively keep their minds on the final prize that is beyond words. He also advises them to keep in mind the place of punishment and correction reserved for those who prefer wrongdoing.*

LET US RETURN again to the same point we were discussing at the beginning. We should not admit everything without discrimination; instead, we should only accept what is useful. For it is shameful to reject foods that are harmful yet to take no thought about the learning that nourishes the soul and, instead, to rush on like a mountain torrent, sweeping everything it happens upon.

[2] And consider: if a ship's captain does not randomly deliver his vessel over to the winds without a plan, but he steers the ship directly to port, or if an archer shoots at a target, or, also, if some bronzesmith or carpenter strives for the end proper to his craft, then what reason would there be for us to be less than such practitioners in terms of the ability to generally perceive our own interests?

[3] For how is it possible that those who work with their hands have some end in view in their own work, but when it comes to

human life, there is no goal for which a man should do and say everything in order not to wholly resemble irrational animals? If there were no intellect guiding our souls, then we would be like ships without ballast, carried everywhere and nowhere throughout life, without a plan or a purpose.

[4] But that's not the way it is. Instead, we should see our lives more in terms of athletic contests, or, if you prefer, music competitions. The competitors prepare themselves with practice exercises for the former contests in which crowns are offered. No one training for a wrestling or a pankration match would practice for a lyre or flute playing competition. [5] Certainly Polydamas did no such thing. Rather, before the contest at Olympia, he practiced bringing speeding chariots to a stop, and by this means he built up the strength of his body.[1] And even though he was pushed and shoved, Milo could not be driven away from his oiled shield. Instead, he firmly held on to it even as a statue is fastened to its base with lead.[2] [6] In short, the training prepared them for their contests. Would these men have soon won crowns or a glorious reputation, or would they have escaped the ridicule of people laughing at their physical condition if they had abandoned the dust and exercises of the gymnasium and wasted their time on practicing the flute of Marsyas or Olympus the Phrygian?

[7] On the other hand, Timotheus the musician certainly did not quit singing in order to spend his time in the wrestling schools. If he had, there's no way he could have surpassed everyone in music in such a way that whenever he wished to he could stir the feelings of a man with an intense and harsh mode or relax them once again with a mode that was serene and calm. [8] It was with this skill that once, when Timotheus was playing the Phrygian mode on his flute to Alexander, he caused the general—as it is said—to leap up and rush to his arms in the middle of a feast. And then, by relaxing the mode, he brought him back again to his drinking friends.[3] That's how great the power is that is supplied by goal-oriented practice, both in terms of music and athletic competitions.

[9] Since I have mentioned crowns and athletes, let me add that these men endure countless hardships, and increase their strength

by every possible means, and shed rivers of sweat while toiling in the gymnasium, and suffer many blows in the trainer's school, and choose not the tastiest food but that selected by the professional trainer, and so pass their days in every other way, so that before the contest their lives are a preparation and training for the contest. Then, when the moment comes, they strip for the race and undergo every hardship and run every risk in order to win a crown of wild olive or of parsley or of some such thing—all so that they may win the victory and have their name announced by the herald.

[10] And yet prizes so extraordinary in terms of their extent and sublimity are set before us for the life we lead that it is impossible to describe them in words.[4] Will it be possible, then, for us to reach out and take hold of these if we are sleeping day and night and living luxurious lives? [11] To be sure, if laziness were valuable for life, then Sardanapalus would carry off the highest prizes of all when it comes to happiness.[5] Or even Margites would carry them off, if you will, the man who was neither a plowman nor a digger nor anything else useful in life, as Homer has it—if, in fact, the poem is by Homer.

[12] Is there not rather truth in the saying of Pittacus, that "It is hard to be good"?[6] For even though we pass through a great deal of toil and suffering, we nevertheless just barely obtain those goods for which, as I said before, no human goods can serve as a model.

[13] Therefore, we should not be careless or lazy, nor should we exchange our great hope for an ephemeral life of ease—that is, if we do not intend to incur reproach and suffer retribution. By the way, I do not mean some punishment here among human beings—even though that is no small matter to a sensible man. No, I refer to the houses of punishment and correction, whether they are beneath the earth or wherever they may happen to be. [14] In the case of the man who does wrong against his will, some allowance and forgiveness may possibly come from God. But for the man who has deliberately and maliciously chosen an inferior life, there is no excuse or begging off. That man has much more punishment and correction to undergo.[7]

NOTES

[1] For Polydamas, see Pausanias, *Description of Greece* 6.5. Among other fabulous stories (including his barehanded killing of a lion on Mount Olympus), Pausanias reports Polydamas' victory in the pankration in the Olympic games of 408 BC.

[2] For Milo, see ibid 6.14 (though Basil's details are slightly different). Milo won in wrestling six times at the Olympic games and seven at the Pythian games.

[3] See Dio Chrysostom *Oration* 1.1. See also Plutarch, *On the Great Fortune or Virtue of Alexander* 2.2—though here Plutarch tells the story about the musician Antigenides rather than Timotheus.

[4] See 1 Corinthians 9.24-25: "Do you not know that in a race all the runners run, but only one gets the prize? Run in such a way as to get the prize. Everyone who competes in the games goes into strict training. They do it to get a crown that will not last, but we do it to get a crown that will last forever."

[5] Sardanapalus, a late Assyrian ruler (possibly Asshurbanipal), had the reputation in the ancient world for great licentiousness, effeminacy, and laziness. See, for example, Dio Chrysostom's contrast of Alexander (a high-energy man oriented to action) with Sardanapalus (an indulgent man oriented to inaction) in *Oration* 1.2-3.

[6] Pittacus was one of the seven wise men of ancient Greece. See Diogenes Laertius, *Lives and Opinions of Eminent Philosophers* 1.4. The saying, or something very similar, is also found in a fragment of the poet Simonides. See Plato, *Protagoras* 340b-d for a discussion of the saying.

[7] Aside from the locations of punishment mentioned in the Bible (for example, Gehenna and Tartarus in the New Testament—whereas Sheol and Hades, though they appear in the Old and New Testaments, are merely locations of the dead rather than clear places of punishment), Basil may have in mind those locations mentioned by Plato. See, for example, *Gorgias* 523a ff. and *Phaedo* 113d ff.

SOUL CARE

FREEING THE SOUL FROM THE BODY AND THE
DEMANDS OF PLEASURE

IN BRIEF: *Basil counsels that his students' major concern should be the care of their souls. For this reason they should work to free their souls from the passions and desires of the body. They may do this by scorning everything that surpasses necessity. Basil defines necessity, or need, in terms of the requirements of nature rather than other perceived needs, including the demands of pleasure—for certain foods, or clothing, or perfumes, or music, or entertainments, or sex, or wealth, or adulation and reputation. He directs them to care for the body only insofar as it may serve the soul, freeing it to pursue wisdom.*

SO THEN, WHAT are we to do?—someone may ask. What else than to devote ourselves to the care of our souls, keeping all our leisure time free from other things.

[2] For this reason we should not slavishly serve the body any more than is strictly necessary. Instead, we should provide the soul with the best things. Through the wisdom of philosophy we should free the soul as though from a prison from its association with the passions of the body, and, at the same time, we should cultivate the body so that it becomes the master of the passions.[1]

For instance, we must minister to the belly with what is necessary—but not with pleasant foods, necessarily, those delicacies sought after by those who look everywhere for table servants and cooks, scouring every land and sea, like those hauling tribute to a harsh master. This is a deplorable business in which one suffers things that are as unbearable as the punishments of Hades, where the inhabitants are forced to card wool into a fire or fetch water in a sieve and pour it into a perforated jar, experiencing never-ending suffering and toil.²

[3] To spend more time than is necessary on one's hair and clothes is, according to the adage of Diogenes, the sign of those who are unhappy or doing wrong.³ Therefore, the man who pampers his body, making himself pretty, or the one who gets the name of such a man, should be considered just as shameful as the man who sleeps with prostitutes or seduces the wives of other men. [4] For as long as his clothing gives him adequate protection against the cold of winter and the heat of summer, what difference should it make—at least to a sensible man—whether he is dressed in a robe made of fine material or in an inexpensive cloak? [5] Similarly, in all other matters, we must be governed by necessity, only giving to the body as much as is beneficial to the soul. It is no less a reproach to a man—one, at least, who is truly worthy of the name—to be fond of and indulge the body, pampering it and making it pretty, than it is to be sordidly preoccupied with any one of the passions.

[6] To exert oneself zealously in every way so that the body itself may be as beautiful as possible is not the sign of a man who either knows himself or understands the wise precept that "the man is not that which is seen." Rather, each one of us, whoever he is, requires extraordinary wisdom to recognize and know himself. But unless we have purified our minds, knowing ourselves is more impossible than it is for a man with darkened eyes to look up at the sun.

[7] Now, to speak in general terms and in a manner sufficient for your understanding, purification of the soul includes scorning those pleasures that satisfy the senses—refusing to feast your eyes on the mindless exhibitions of jugglers and the like or on the sight of bodies that prompt one to seek pleasure, and closing your ears to songs that pour over and utterly destroy your soul. [8] I say this because those passions that are the offspring of cupidity and depravity are naturally produced by this kind of music. On the other hand, we must pursue the other kind of music, which is better in itself and leads to better things. As the scriptures say, David, the composer of sacred songs, freed the king from his madness. [9] And the story is related that Pythagoras too, when he happened upon

some drunken revelers, commanded the flute player, who led the band of revelers, to change the mode in order to play in the Doric mode. As a result, these returned to their senses thanks to the new mode. And throwing off their garlands, they went home ashamed. [10] Yet others, when they hear the sound of the flute, rave in Corybantic and Bacchic frenzy. Such is the difference between being filled up with healthy versus worthless music. Since this latter kind of music is now in vogue, you should have less to do with it than with other shameful things.[4]

[11] Furthermore, I am ashamed to even have to forbid filling the air with whole clouds of sweet smelling perfumes that carry pleasure to your nose, or to smear your body with creams and lotions.

And what can be said about the importance of not hunting after those pleasures associated with the senses of touch and taste? Such hunting compels those who are devoted to these pleasures to live like wild animals, giving all their attention to the belly and the members below it.

[12] But, in a word, every part of the body should be despised by everyone who does not care to be buried in its pleasures as if in filth. We should attach ourselves to the body only insofar as we receive support from it in the pursuit of wisdom and philosophy. This is as Plato declares, speaking in a manner similar to Paul, who exhorts us to make no provision for the body as a location to satisfy the desires.[5] [13] Is there any difference between those who are anxious to make the body as beautiful as possible but ignore the purpose of the soul as utterly useless, and those who are zealously concerned for their tools but neglect the art by which they work? [14] On the contrary, we should discipline the body and hold it in check, even as we do the violent attacks of an untamed animal. We should quiet the restlessness and confusion produced by the body in the soul with the lash of reason, not giving full rein to pleasure. We should do this instead of relaxing the reins and allowing the mind to be swept along like a charioteer carried on by unmanageable and willful horses.[6]

Keep in mind Pythagoras, who, upon learning that one of his followers was putting on extra weight thanks to all his exercise and excessive eating, said to him, "Are you not making your imprisonment more difficult for yourself?"

[15] There's also the story that Plato, in order to defend against the harmful influence of the body, deliberately occupied the Academy, which is the pestilential part of Attica, so that he could rid himself of excessive bodily comfort even as one prunes the vine of excessive growth. I myself have heard physicians say that one can take "good health" to an extreme, even to the point of danger.

[16] Since, then, such excessive care for the body is not only unprofitable for the body but also an impediment to the soul, the idea that the soul should be subject to the body as its servant is sheer madness!

[17] But surely, if we make it our practice to look down on the body, taking no notice of it, we will hardly admire anything other men possess. After all, what use will we have for wealth if we scorn the pleasures that come through the body? As for me, I see no use— unless there is, as with the dragons found in legends, some pleasure in guarding hidden treasure!

[18] Surely, however, the man who has been brought up to be free of this sort of thing will not likely prefer anything base or shameful in word or deed. For such a man will scorn that which surpasses need—even if it is the gold dust of Lydia or the product of the gold gathering ants.[7] As his need for the thing decreases, his scorn for its excessive use will increase. And doubtlessly he will define "need" itself in terms of the necessary requirements of nature, and not in terms of pleasure.

[19] Those who go beyond the bounds of necessity resemble people who rush headlong down a slope. They are unable to grab hold of anything to stop their precipitous fall. No, the more they grasp at things, the more things they need to satisfy the desires.

This accords with Solon, the son of Execestides, who declares, "As for wealth, no one has made its limits clear to men."[8]

[20] We should also resort to Theognis as a teacher on this point, when he says, "I do not desire wealth, nor do I pray for it; rather, may it be mine to live on little, suffering no misfortune."[9]

I also admire the disdain that Diogenes had without exception for every human good. He declared himself wealthier than the

Great King since he needed less for living.[10] [21] Even so, for those of us alive today, it would seem that nothing is enough to satisfy us apart from the money of Pythias the Mysian, and such a great quantity of land, and cattle herds beyond counting.[11]

Nevertheless, I believe that we should not yearn after wealth when it is absent. And if it is nearby, we should not make it our purpose to possess it as much as we should to dispose of it well.[12] [22] In this regard, Socrates' saying is well put. When a wealthy man was expressing great pride in all his possessions, Socrates told him that he would not admire him before he had learned whether or not the man knew how to use his wealth.[13] [23] Would not Pheidias and Polykleitos—the one who made the Zeus for the Elians, and the other the Hera for the Argives—have been the objects of derision for glorying in a wealth not their own if they had greatly prided themselves on the gold and ivory in the statues rather than the art that enabled them to render the gold both more pleasing and valuable? In view of that, do we not deserve just as much shame if we believe that human virtue is insufficient in itself to serve as an adornment for us?

[24] Moreover, are we to despise wealth and scorn the pleasures of the senses and yet go on seeking after flattery and adulation, vying with the fox of Archilochus in cunning and craft?[14] [25] On the contrary, there is nothing that a prudent man should flee more than living for praise and worrying about what everyone thinks. Instead, he should make sound reason the guide of his life so that—even if he must speak against all other men and risk their contempt for the sake of what is noble—he will not at all shift away from that which he knows to be right. [26] Otherwise, how will we say that he differs from the Egyptian sophist, who, whenever he wished, became a plant, or a wild animal, or fire, or water, or anything else?[15] [27] Just as the flatterer does, such a man now praises justice to those who honor it, and now goes on in an opposite manner when he senses that injustice is popular. And just as the octopus, they say, changes its color to match the ground upon which it rests, so does this man change his mind according to the opinions of those around him.

NOTES

[1] For the idea that the body is the prison of the soul, and for the soul's release, see Plato's *Phaedo* 64b-c, 67c-d, and 82e-83a.

[2] According to N.G. Wilson, these are "three proverbial expressions describing the punishments . . . in Hades" (*Saint Basil on Greek Literature*, 64). See Plato, *Laws* 6.780c-d, and Lucian, *Dialogue of the Dead* 11.4.

[3] The "Diogenes" here is the Cynic Diogenes of Sinope. See Diogenes Laertius, *Lives and Opinions of Eminent Philosophers* 6.54: "Seeing a young man beautifying himself, [Diogenes] said, 'If it is for men, you are unfortunate. If it is for women, you do wrong.'" For an introduction to Cynic teachings, themes, and ideas, see *The Cynics: Cynic Philosophy for Desiring, Enduring & Living Well* (Sugar Land: The Classics Cave, 2020) or *The Best of the Cynics* (Sugar Land: The Classics Cave, 2020).

[4] For David, see 1 Samuel 16.14-23. For Socrates' discussion of music and its different modes and moral effects, see Plato, *Republic* 3.398 ff.

[5] See Plato, *Republic* 6.498b-c; and Romans 13.14: "Put on the Lord Jesus Christ, and make no provision for the flesh, to gratify its desires."

[6] Compare Plato's *Phaedrus* 253c-e.

[7] Herodotus tells the story of the gold gathering ants in *Histories* 3.102 ff.

[8] Solon, *Elegies* 13.71.

[9] Theognis 1155-6.

[10] The reference is to the Cynic Diogenes of Sinope. See Plutarch, *On the Fortune and Virtue of Alexander* 1.10.

[11] According to Herodotus, Pythias was a Lydian of great wealth (*Histories* 7.27 ff.).

[12] For a similar early view on the use of wealth, see Clement of Alexandria's *The Rich Man's Salvation*.

[13] See, for instance, Dio Chrysostom, *Oration* 3.1 ff., where Socrates reserves judgment regarding "the Persian king" Darius. See also, Cicero, *Tusculan Disputations* 5.12.

[14] The reference is to the seventh century BC poet Archilochus of Paros and the fable he told about the fox and the eagle. See Plato, *Republic* 2.365c.

[15] The reference is to the shapeshifter Proteus in Homer, *Odyssey* 4.384-386; 417-418. Proteus is called "the Egyptian sophist" in Plato, *Euthydemus* 288b.

GATHERING SUPPLIES FOR THE JOURNEY
THE TIME TO ACT IS NOW

IN BRIEF: *Basil explains the usefulness of gathering together non-Christian writings having to do with virtue. Even though Christian writings are superior to these, he affirms that the many small advantages coming from such non-Christian writings can add up to a great benefit. The goal is to gather supplies for the journey of life—not only for this present life, as with Bias, but for eternity. In short, his students should always choose what is best. They should act now rather than letting the condition of their souls become so bad that they despair.*

EVEN THOUGH WE will learn all these things more completely and perfectly in our own writings, nevertheless, for the present let us draw a kind of rough sketch, as it were, of what virtue is according to outside teachings.

Those who make it their business to collect whatever is beneficial from every writing are like rivers that grow larger by taking in the flow of streams from every side. [2] The poet's saying about "adding little to little" is true not only for the accumulation of money but also for gathering together every kind of knowledge.[1]

[3] Take Bias, for example. When his son was about to depart for Egypt, he asked his father what he could do that would most please him, and Bias replied, "Acquire traveling supplies for your old age."[2] By "traveling supplies" he doubtlessly meant virtue, even though he defined virtue in terms that were far too narrow since he limited virtue's benefit to human life.

[4] As for me, if anyone mentions the old age of Tithonos, or that of Arganthonios, or of Mathusala, whose life was the longest of any man's life (since he is said to have lived a thousand years less

thirty), or if anyone carefully measures all the time that has elapsed since human beings have existed, I will laugh as though at the notions of children, since I look forward to that long and ageless eternity whose limit the mind can no more grasp than it can hypothesize an end for the immortal soul.[3] [5] I would exhort you to acquire traveling supplies for this long age, leaving no stone unturned, as the proverb has it, wherever you may discover some benefit toward that end.

Let us not shrink from this task because it is difficult and onerous. Rather, let us remember the words of the man who urged everyone to choose the life that is in itself best, in the expectation that this life will become agreeable when we make a habit of it.[4] Accordingly, let us try for the best things. [6] For it would be shameful to squander this present season only to beg for it later on while in distress, when there will be no more time.

[7] So then, of the things I judge most excellent, I have mentioned some now, while I will continue to advise you regarding other things throughout my whole life.

As for you, remember that there are three kinds of patients with varying degrees of illness. You do not want to be as the one who is incurable, being sick in mind like the one who is unfortunate in his body. [8] For whereas those who suffer from small maladies go by themselves to a physician, and those who are attacked by more serious illnesses summon care to their own homes, those who reach the stage of despondency, where the illness is absolutely incurable, do not even admit a physician when he calls.

I pray now that you may not suffer in this way by shunning those whose writings are sound.

NOTES

[1] See Hesiod, *Works and Days* 361 ff.

[2] Bias was one of the seven wise men of ancient Greece. See Diogenes Laertius, *Lives and Opinions of Eminent Philosophers* 1.88: "Make wisdom your provision for the journey from youth to old age; for it is a more certain support than all other possessions."

[3] For Tithonus, who was tragically granted immortality without agelessness,

see *Homeric Hymn to Aphrodite* 5.218 ff.; for Arganthonios, who is reported to have lived 120 years, see Herodotus, *Histories* 1.163 (Lucian, however, reported 150 years; see Lucian, *Macrobioi* 10); for Mathusala, who is said to have lived 969 years (Basil rounds this to 970), see Genesis 5.27.

[4] See Plutarch, *On Exile* 8: "That goad precept of the Pythagoreans, 'Make choice of the best life you can and custom will make it pleasant,' is here also wise and useful."

PART 2
Basil and Literature

- Other Texts from Basil Related to
Education and Greek Literature

- Select Literature Referenced
or Suggested By Basil

OTHER TEXTS FROM BASIL RELATED TO
EDUCATION AND GREEK LITERATURE

The following texts—all from Basil's letters—offer evidence of Basil's use of literature, both Christian and non-Christian alike, in education and living life. Clearly, his approach is no straightforward one. Rather, his is that of the bee or the gardener found in his address on how to benefit from reading Greek literature (see 4.7-9).[1]

LETTER 74 *to Martinianus alludes to Odysseus, the well-travelled and knowledgeable man. It mentions the episode in Homer's* Odyssey *when the Phaeacian ruler Alcinous announces his pleasure in listening to Odysseus tell the stories of his adventures. The underlying emphasis is the benefit of learning about the good and beautiful and about virtue.*

HOW HIGH DO you suppose one to prize the pleasure of our meeting each other once again? How delightful to spend a longer time with you so as to enjoy all your good qualities! If powerful proof is given of culture in seeing many men's ways, such I am sure is quickly given in your society. For what is the difference between seeing many men singly or one who has gained experience of all together? I should say that there is an immense superiority in that which gives the knowledge of good and beautiful things without trouble and puts within our reach instruction in virtue, pure from all admixture of evil. Is there question of noble deed; of words worth handing down; of institutions of men of superhuman excellence? All are treasured in the storehouse of your mind. I would not pray, then, to listen to you only for a year—as Alcinous to Odysseus— but throughout my whole life.[2]

In LETTER 4 *to Olympius, we observe positive references to the early Cynics and Stoics and see that Basil doubtlessly admires and has learned from both schools of philosophy. It should be noted, by the way, that much of*

Basil's writings on asceticism and Christian practice echoes earlier Cynic teachings. See, for instance, Letter 223, where Basil introduces many Cynic themes (chosen poverty, "self-control," "endurance in toil," ragged clothing, "a life of endurance," and so on).[3]

WHAT DO YOU mean, my excellent man, by evicting Poverty from our retreat—Poverty, my dear friend and the nurse of philosophy? If she were but gifted with speech, I take it you would have to appear as a defendant in an action for unlawful eviction. She might plead as follows: "I chose to live with this man Basil, an admirer of Zeno [of Citium], who, when he had lost everything in a shipwreck, cried with great fortitude, 'Well done, Fortune! You are reducing me to a worn out cloak.' He's also a great admirer of Cleanthes [of Assos], who, by drawing water from the well, got enough to live on and pay his tutors' fees as well. Moreover, he's an immense admirer of Diogenes [of Sinope], who prided himself on requiring no more than was absolutely necessary, and flung away his bowl after he had learned from some lad to stoop down and drink from the hollow of his hand.[4]

LETTER 8 *to the Caesareans (long before Basil was their bishop) presents Basil as defending the orthodox Christian position against the Arians— "the Philistines"—who have inappropriately introduced ideas from Greek philosophy. This means that however much one may benefit from Greek philosophy (and Basil believes one can, particularly relative to ethics), one must not accept it wholesale.*

FRIENDS GODLY AND well beloved—I implore you to be aware of the shepherds of the Philistines. Do not let them unexpectedly choke your wills. Let them not befoul the purity of your knowledge of the faith. This is always their goal—not to teach simple souls lessons drawn from sacred Scripture, but to mar the harmony of the truth by outside wisdom and philosophy. Is he not an open Philistine who is introducing the terms *unbegotten* and *begotten* into our faith?

LETTER 294 *to Festus and Magnus explains the importance of literature from the past. In it we receive instruction from those who lived long ago.*

Basil also sounds the note that our emphasis should be on the care of our souls.

NOT THAT SEPARATION in the body is a hindrance to instruction. The creator, in the fullness of his love and wisdom, did not confine our minds within our bodies or the power of speaking to our tongues. Ability to profit derives some advantage even from a lapse of time; therefore, we are able to transmit instruction not only to those who are dwelling far away but even to those who eventually will be born. And experience proves my words: those who lived many years ago teach posterity by instruction preserved in their writings. And we, though so far separated in the body, are always near in thought and converse together with ease. Instruction is limited neither by sea nor land, if only we care for our souls' profit.

In LETTER *223 "against Eustathius of Sebasteia," Basil renounces the "wisdom made foolish by God," that is, human philosophy, echoing Saint Paul's thoughts in his Letter to the Corinthians. Following his renunciation, he describes his conversion to the light of the Gospel in words reminiscent of Plato's allegory of the cave. Interestingly, much of Basil's letter (though not presented below) has very strong Cynic accents in that he highlights his turn toward chosen poverty, "self-control," "endurance in toil," ragged clothing, "a life of endurance," and so on.*

MUCH TIME HAD I spent in vanity. I had wasted nearly all my youth in the vain labor that I underwent in acquiring the wisdom made foolish by God. Then once upon a time, like a man roused from deep sleep, I turned my eyes to the marvelous light of the truth of the Gospel, and I perceived the uselessness of the wisdom of the princes of this world that comes to nothing.[5]

In LETTER *2 to Gregory of Nazianzus, Basil explains the significance of studying the sacred Scriptures. Note the emphasis on the examples of good men—in this case for "finding our duty" and living a good life. It is the same emphasis we find in Basil's advice relative to reading Greek literature. The examples here are Joseph, Job, David, and Moses.*

THE STUDY OF inspired Scripture is the chief way of finding our duty, for in it we find delivered in writing both instruction about conduct and the lives of blessed men, as some breathing images of godly living, for the imitation of their good works. Hence, in whatever respect each one feels himself deficient, devoting himself to this imitation, he finds, as from some dispensary, the due medicine for his ailment.

He who is a lover of moderation and chastity dwells upon the history of Joseph, and from him learns moderate and chaste actions, finding him not only possessed of self-command over pleasure but virtuously-minded in habit.

He is taught endurance by Job, who, not only when the circumstances of life began to turn against him—in one moment he was plunged from wealth into penury, and from being the father of fair children into childlessness—did he remain the same, keeping the disposition of his soul all through uncrushed, but he was not even stirred to anger against the friends who came to comfort him and trampled on him and aggravated his troubles.

Or if he inquires how to be at once gentle and great-hearted, hearty against sin, meek and gentle toward men, he will find David noble in warlike exploits yet gentle and unruffled relative to revenge against enemies.

Such, too, was Moses rising up with great heart upon sinners against God but with a gentle soul bearing their evil-speaking against himself.

Thus, generally, as painters, when they are painting from other pictures, constantly look at the model and do their best to transfer its lineaments to their own work, so too must he who is desirous of rendering himself perfect in all branches of excellence keep his eyes turned to the lives of the saints, as though to living and moving statues, and make their virtue his own by imitation.[6]

In LETTER 41 *to the emperor Julian, his onetime fellow student and friend, Basil recalls the extent of their learning together. The latter part hints at Julian's turn from Christianity to the old Greek religion.*

I CONSIDER HOW you and I have learned together the lessons of the best and holiest literature. Each of us went through the sacred and God-inspired Scriptures. Then nothing was hid from you. Nowadays you have become lost to proper feeling, beleaguered as you are with pride.[7]

In LETTER 42 *to his student Chilo, Basil recommends and discusses the value, and possible challenges, of studying the Old and New Testaments of the Bible. The relative value of any given text—though in itself it may be judged objectively valuable—oftentimes depends on the reader.*

NEVER NEGLECT READING—especially of the New Testament. I say this because very frequently mischief comes of reading the Old. It's not that what is written is harmful but that the minds of the injured are weak. All bread is nutritious, but it may be injurious to the sick. Just so all scripture is God-inspired and profitable, and there is nothing in it unclean.[8]

In LETTER 339 *to the sophist and his one-time teacher Libanius, Basil explains that he has shifted his attention to the men found in the sacred scriptures of the Christian Church rather than other teachings from others sources. Nevertheless, he recognizes the difference in the quality of writing between what he is reading and Greek literature.*

HOWEVER, MY EXCELLENT man, I am now spending my time with Moses and Elijah and blessed men like them, who tell me their stories in a barbarous tongue, and I utter what I learned from them, true, indeed, in sense, though rude in phrase, as what I am writing testifies. If ever I learned anything from you, I have forgotten it in the course of time.

The next set of passages indicates how Basil referenced Greek literature in his own writings. They demonstrate how his own mind was saturated with the people, images, and ideas of ancient Greece.

In LETTER 14 *to his friend Gregory of Nazianzus, Basil describes his spiritual retreat, comparing it to Calypso's island.*

I DEPARTED INTO Pontus in quest of a place to live in. There God has opened on me a spot exactly answering to my taste, so that I actually see before my eyes what I have often pictured to my mind in idle fancy.

There is a lofty mountain covered with thick woods, watered toward the north with cool and transparent streams. A plain lies beneath, enriched by the waters that are ever draining off from it, and skirted by a spontaneous profusion of trees almost thick enough to be a fence—so as even to surpass Calypso's island, which Homer seems to have considered the most beautiful spot on earth.[9] Indeed it is like an island, enclosed as it is on all sides. For deep hollows cut off two sides of it. The river, which has lately fallen down a precipice, runs all along the front and is impassable as a wall. The mountain, extending itself behind and meeting the hollows in a crescent, stops up the path at its roots. There is but one pass—and I am master of it. . . .

The chief praise of the place is, that being happily disposed for produce of every kind, it nurtures what to me is the sweetest produce of all—quietness. In fact it is not only rid of the bustle of the city but it is even unfrequented by travelers, except for a chance hunter. It abounds in game, as well as other things—but not, I am glad to say, in bears or wolves, such as you have, but in deer, wild goats, hares, and the like.

Does it not strike you what a foolish mistake I was near making when I was eager to change this spot for your Tiberina, the very pit of the whole earth? Pardon me, then, if I am now set on it. For not Alcmaeon himself, I suppose, could endure to wander further when he had found the Echinades.[10]

In LETTER 74 *to Martinianus Basil references the tragedy of Pentheus' violent death from Euripides'* Bacchae, *when he, the king of Thebes, is torn apart by Maenads.*

MY COUNTRY IN her troubles calls me irresistibly to her side. You know, my friend, how she suffers. She is torn to pieces like Pentheus by actual Maenads, daemons. They are dividing her and dividing her again. . . .[11]

In another portion of LETTER 74, *Basil mentions the poet Simonides and the playwright Aeschylus as poets who are skilled in expressing trouble and calamity.*

I WISH IT were possible for you to come yourself among us and actually see our deplorable situation! . . . Truly, we want some Simonides, or another similar poet, to lament our troubles from actual experience. But why name Simonides? I should instead mention Aeschylus or any other who has depicted a great calamity in words like his, and uttered lamentation with a mighty voice.[12]

In LETTER 83 *to a magistrate, Basil hints at Aristotle's teaching regarding friendship.*

I HAVE A property at Chamanene, and I beg you to look after its interests as though they were your own. And do not be surprised at my calling my friend's property my own, for among other virtues I have been taught that of friendship. And I remember the wise author of the wise saying that a friend is another self.[13]

In LETTER 112 *to Andronicus, a general, Basil advises the recipient to be merciful to a man called Domitian. Why? Because, he says, "those who surpassed their fellows in philosophy did not persist in their wrath." Therefore Andronicus should quit his anger against Domitian in the manner of Croesus, the king of Lydia, who "ceased his wrath against the slayer of his son," and in the manner of Cyrus the Great, who "was friendly to this very Croesus after his victory" over him. Both stories are recounted in Herodotus'* Histories.

LET THE FEAR Domitian has of what he suspects, and of what he knows he deserves to suffer, be the extent of his chastisement. I entreat you to add nothing to his punishment. For consider this: many in former times, of whom no record has reached us, have had those who wronged them in their power. But those who surpassed their fellows in philosophy did not persist in their wrath. And of these the memory has been handed down, immortal through all time. Let this glory be added to what history will say of you. Grant to us, who desire to celebrate your praises, to be able to go beyond the instances of kindness sung of in the days of old. In this manner Croesus, it is said, ceased from his wrath against the slayer of his son, when he gave himself up for punishment. And the great Cyrus was friendly to this very Croesus after his victory. We shall number you with these and shall proclaim this your glory with all our power.[14]

LETTERS 147 *and* 148 *refer to Homer. In* 147 *to Aburgius, Basil compares the fall of Odysseus, when he was* "*stripped of everything,*" *to that of Maximus, the former prefect of his homeland.* "*Maximus was governor of no insignificant people, just as Odysseus was chief of the Cephallenians.*" *Now, he reports, Maximus has fallen from power and wealth to* "*undeserved misfortune*" —*and all because* "*he has provoked some Laestrygonian . . . and fallen in with some Scylla . . . since he has barely been able to swim out of this inextricable whirlpool.*" *In* LETTER 148 *to Trajan, Basil mentions* "*the* Iliad *of misfortune in which Maximus is involved*" —*the reference being to the immense amount of, as Homer puts it,* "*pain and suffering among the Achaeans.*" [15]

UP TO THIS time I used to think Homer a fable, when I read the second part of his poem, in which he narrates the adventures of Odysseus. But the calamity that has befallen the most excellent Maximus has led me to look on what I used to think fabulous and incredible, as exceedingly probable. Maximus was governor of no insignificant people just as Odysseus was chief of the Cephallenians. Odysseus had had great wealth and returned stripped of everything. To such straits has calamity reduced Maximus, that he may have to present himself at home in borrowed rags. And perhaps he has suffered all this because he has provoked some Laestrygonian against him, and has fallen in with some Scylla, hiding a dog's fierceness and fury under a woman's form. Since then he has barely been able to swim out of this inextricable whirlpool.[16]

In LETTER 151 *to Eustathius the physician, Basil quotes a general Stoic teaching.*

THE PHRASE OF the Stoics runs, "Since things do not happen as we wish them to happen, then we wish them to happen as they do."[17]

LETTER 186 finds Basil praising philosophy to the governor Antipater.

PHILOSOPHY IS AN excellent thing, if only for this, that it heals its disciples at a small cost. For in philosophy the same thing is both a relish and healthy fare.[18]

In LETTER 189 to Eustathius the physician, Basil recounts a story told by Aesop in order to explain the "unexpected attitude of hatred" of his opponents against him.

IN ADOPTING AN unexpected attitude of hatred against me, my opponents seem to be repeating the old story in Aesop.[19] He makes the wolf bring certain charges against the lamb, as being really ashamed to seem to kill a creature who had done him no harm without some reasonable pretext. Then, when the lamb easily rebuts the slander, the wolf nonetheless continues his attack, and, though defeated relative to fairness, he wins by biting. Just so with those who seem to count hatred as a virtue. They will perhaps blush to hate me without a cause, and so they invent pleas and charges against me without standing by any of their allegations. Instead, as the ground of their detestation, they put forward now this, now that, and now something else.

In LETTER 272 to Sophronius, Basil refers to Alexander the Great and the time he trusted his physician with his life as a way of asking Sophronius to trust him.

YOU MUST NOT refuse to believe what I say, unless you regard me as quite a desperate character, who thinks nothing of the great sin of lying. Put away all suspicion of me in relation to the business, and for the future reckon my affection for you as beyond the reach of calumny. Imitate Alexander. He received a letter saying that his physician was plotting his death at the very moment when he was just about to drink his medicine. Even so, he was so far from believing the slanderer that he at one and the same time read the letter and drank the dose of medicine.[20]

In LETTER 334 *to "a writer," Basil—as it were—channels an elementary school teacher, instructing the recipient in the best way to form letters so that a reader will have an easier time following his writing (hint: the lines of each letter should be straight rather than slanting "like Aesop's crab"). Basil compares his own experience of reading the recipient's writing to the story of Theseus, who had to follow "Ariadne's thread" in order to find her. The conclusion? "Write straight, and do not confuse our mind by your slanted and irregular writing."*

WRITE STRAIGHT, AND make the lines straight. . . . Avoid forcing the pen to travel slantwise, like Aesop's crab. Advance straight on, as if following the line of the carpenter's rule, which always preserves exactitude and prevents any irregularity. The oblique is ungraceful. It is the straight that pleases the eye and does not allow the reader's eyes to go nodding up and down like a swing-beam. This has been my fate in reading your writing. As the lines lie in the manner of a ladder, I was obliged, when I had to go from one to another, to mount up to the end of the last. Then, when no connection was to be found, I had to go back and seek for the right order again, retreating and following the furrow, like Theseus in the story following Ariadne's thread.[21] Write straight, and do not confuse our mind by your slanting and irregular writing.

LETTER 348 *to Libanius has many references to things Greek—to the* "sophist ingenuity [that Libanius] has got from the depths of Plato"; *to the* "tribe of sophists, whose craft is to make money out of their words"; *to the battle of Thermopylae* ("I have ordered as many rafters to be supplied as there were fighters at Thermopylae" —*that is, 300); and to Homer's term* "long-shadowing."[22]

LETTER 359, *also to Libanius, mentions "the art of the ancients," and that, if it were possible, Basil "would have made for himself Icarus' wings and come to you" if only "the art of Daedalus" had been safe.*

YOU, WHO HAVE included all the art of the ancients in your own mind, are so silent that you do not even let me get any gain in a letter. I, if the art of Daedalus had only been safe, would have made Icarus' wings for me and come to you. But wax cannot be entrusted to the sun, and so, instead of Icarus' wings, I send you words to prove my affection.[23]

NOTES

[1] Letter passages are from the translation (sometimes modified) found in Blomfield Jackson, *St. Basil: Letters and Select Works*, vol. 8 of *The Nicene and Post-Nicene Fathers* (Grand Rapids: WM.B. Eerdmans Publishing Co., 1894).

[2] See Homer, *Odyssey* 11.355-376.

[3] Admittedly, many of these themes are also found in the life of Jesus and the remainder of the New Testament. For an introduction to Cynic teachings, themes, and ideas, see *The Cynics: Cynic Philosophy for Desiring, Enduring & Living Well* (Sugar Land: The Classics Cave, 2020) or *The Best of the Cynics* (Sugar Land: The Classics Cave, 2020).

[4] Zeno of Citium was the founder of the Stoics. He was originally a student of Crates, the Cynic philosopher. Cleanthes followed Zeno as the head of the Stoic school. For more on ancient Stoicism, its teachings, and approach to the good life, see *Early Stoicism: Stoic Philosophy for Living Well & Happiness — Ancient Stoic Writings & Accounts of Stoicism* or *The Best of Early Stoicism* (Sugar Land: The Classics Cave, 2020). Diogenes of Sinope was the founder of the Cynics, more a way of life than a school (or at least that is what some judged in the ancient world). The three anecdotes may be found in Diogenes Laertes, *Lives and Opinions of Eminent Philosophers* 7.2-5 (Zeno of Citium); 7.168-170 (Cleanthes of Assos); 6.37 (Diogenes of Sinope). On the Cynic counsel to welcome Poverty as guard of one's house, see Diogenes' *Letter 36* to Timomachus.

[5] Compare to 1 Corinthians 3.19. For the allegory, see Plato, *Republic* 7.514a-517b.

[6] Compare to Basil, *How to Benefit from Reading Greek Literature* 6.2.

[7] For an account of Julian's turn, see Polymnia Athanassiadi, *Julian: An Intellectual Biography* (Oxford: Oxford University Press, 1981).

[8] See 2 Timothy 3.16: "All Scripture is God-inspired and is useful for teaching, rebuking, correcting, and training in righteousness." The saying that "all bread is nutritious . . ." may equally have been applied by Basil to non-Christian literature.

⁹ For the lush natural beauty of Calypso's island, see Homer, *Odyssey* 5.63-75, where Hermes comes to her island and marvels.

¹⁰ According to the story given in Apollodorus' *Library*, after murdering his mother, Eriphyle, Alcmaeon was "visited by the Fury of his mother's murder" and grew mad. He eventually found purification and sanity when he made his way to the Achelous River and the Echinades islands built up by the river's deposit of silt.

¹¹ See Euripides, *Bacchae* 1114-1136, which in part reads, "Agave . . . tore off his arm at the shoulder. . . . Pentheus moaned and groaned. . . . . One woman carried off an arm while another snatched a foot with its boot. His naked ribs were visible when the skin was torn from his side. And everyone, with bloody hands, played a game of catch with Pentheus' flesh. His body was scattered under rugged rocks and amid the luxuriant foliage of the woods. It will not be easy to find all the parts."

¹² Basil is likely thinking of Simonides' famous epitaph for the fallen Spartan soldiers, who heroically defended and died at the narrow pass at Thermopylae in 480 BC. As for Aeschylus, all of his surviving plays, among them the three plays constituting the *Oresteia*, explore the various faces of suffering.

¹³ See Aristotle, *Nicomachean Ethics* 9.4.5 (1166a).

¹⁴ See Herodotus, *Histories* 1.45 and 1.88.

¹⁵ See Homer, *Iliad* 1.2.

¹⁶ See Homer, *Odyssey* 10.105-132 (for the Laestrygonians) and 12.85-126; 234-258 (for Scylla and the whirlpool Charybdis).

¹⁷ More specifically, the saying comes from Epictetus: "Do not seek to have everything that happens happen as you wish, but wish for everything to happen as it actually does happen, and your life will be serene" (*Handbook* 8).

¹⁸ Though Basil's statement is not a reference to a specific author, the idea that philosophy heals is general among ancient philosophers. For a paean to philosophy, see Cicero, *Tusculan Disputations* 5.5 ff.

¹⁹ For the story of the wolf and the lamb, see Aesop, *Fables* 155 (numbered according to the Perry Index).

²⁰ For the account, see Plutarch, *Alexander* 19.

²¹ For the story of Theseus and Ariadne, see Ovid, *Metamorphoses* Book 8.

²² Basil likely has Plato's *Cratylus* in mind ("from the depths of Plato"). For the battle of Thermopylae, see Herodotus, *Histories* 7. The term *dolichoskios* (long-shadowing or casting a long shadow) is found in both Homer's *Iliad* and *Odyssey*. For example, see *Iliad* 3.346 or *Odyssey* 19.438.

²³ For the story of Daedalus and Icarus, see Ovid, *Metamorphoses* Book 8.

SELECT LITERATURE
REFERENCED OR SUGGESTED BY BASIL

Basil directly refers to or indirectly hints at a large number of ancient authors and literature. The following selections present some of the authors and passages that were likely in Basil's mind, as well as brief explanations of Basil's use and their original significance.

Before getting to the passages themselves, we should be aware that Basil's use and interpretation of a passage is sometimes slightly, if not wholly, different from the evident meaning of the passage. Such a practice was not uncommon for his age. Also, his citation of a text is at times slightly different from the original words of the text.

THE BIBLE   *Moses was wise*

Let's begin with the stories of Moses and Daniel. Basil claims that both studied wisdom that was not directly related to the "divine teachings" of the Christian tradition. "They say, moreover, that even Moses—that most excellent man whose name for wisdom is greatest among all mankind—exercised his mind in the knowledge of the Egyptians, and in this way he approached the contemplation of the one Who Is. They similarly affirm that the wise man Daniel—though in later times—closely examined and thoroughly learned the wisdom of the Chaldeans before partaking in the divine teachings." [1] *The following are the passages that Basil must have had in mind. The first two, having to do with Moses' education and God's self-revelation to Moses, are from the Acts of the Apostles and the Book of Exodus.*

MOSES WAS EDUCATED in all the wisdom of the Egyptians and was powerful in speech and action.[2]

GOD SAID TO Moses, "I am Who I Am." This is what you are to say to the Israelites: "I Am has sent me to you."[3]

The final passage from the Book of Daniel has to do with the prophet Daniel's education. It relates how Ashpenaz, the leading man of king Nebuchadnezzar's court officials, was to select young men from the nobility of the Israelites to educate. Daniel was one of the chosen young men.

HE WAS TO teach them the literature and language of the Babylonians . . . for three years . . . [so that they could] enter the king's service.[4]

PLATO

In response to the question, "So then, what are we to do?" that "someone may ask," Basil responds in a manner that Plato (and Socrates) would have been quite pleased with. "What else than to devote ourselves to the care of our souls, keeping all our leisure time free from other things." [5] *The response echoes Socrates' bold statement to the Athenians during his trial, that we are to care most for our souls, for wisdom, truth, and virtue.*

Socrates speaking "MEN OF ATHENS, I greet and love you, but I will obey the god rather than you. And while I live and am able to continue, I will never give up philosophy. Nor will I stop exhorting you and pointing out the truth to any one of you whom I happen to encounter. Rather, in my accustomed way, I will say, "Best of men, you who are a citizen of Athens, the greatest of cities and the most famous for wisdom and power—are you not ashamed to care for the acquisition of the most wealth possible, and for reputation and honor, when you neither care for nor worry about practical wisdom and truth and your soul, that it may be in the best possible condition? And if any of you disagrees, saying that he *does* care, then I will not let him go, nor will I go. But I will question him. I will examine and cross-examine him. And if it appears to me that he does not possess virtue, but he says he does, I will upbraid him for devaluing the highest things and valuing the lowest."[6]

How does Basil suggest that we care for our souls? "Through philosophy," he says, "we should free the soul as though from a prison from its association with the passions of the body, and, at the same time, we should cultivate the body so that it becomes the master of the passions." [7] The advice duplicates much of what Plato (through Socrates) says in the Phaedo.

Socrates speaking "NOW, GOOD MAN, see if you agree with me. . . . Does it appear to you that a man who practices philosophy will be eager about the so-called pleasures—those such as eating and drinking?"

"Not at all, Socrates," Simmias said.

"And what about the pleasures related to sex?"

"Certainly not."

"And what about these? Does it seem to you that he will esteem the other pleasures related to the care of the body—those, for instance, such as the possession of fine clothes and sandals and other embellishments for the body? What's your view? Will he think highly of them or scorn them unless they are absolutely necessary for him to have?"

"It seems to me," he said, "that the true philosopher will scorn them."

"Generally, then," Socrates said, "it seems to you that such a man is not occupied with the affairs of the body. Instead, he abandons it insofar as he is able and orients himself to the soul."

"That's how it seems to me."

"So then, above all it is clear that in such matters the philosopher, more than other men, frees the soul as much as possible from its association with the body?"

"It appears so."[8]

Later on, Socrates discusses philosophy as the means by which the soul is released from the prison of the body.

Socrates speaking "THOSE WHO CARE for their own souls and do not live in service to the body dismiss all these men [who have lived viciously] and do not walk in their ways since they did not know where they were going or in what manner. They themselves hold that one should not do anything contrary to philosophy—to the freedom and catharsis it provides. And so they turn and follow the way of philosophy wherever it leads."

"How do they do this, Socrates?"

"I will tell you," he said. "The lovers of learning know that when philosophy first takes possession of their soul it is entirely fastened and welded to the body and is compelled to contemplate realities through the body as through prison bars, not with its own unhindered vision, and is wallowing in utter ignorance. And philosophy sees that the most dreadful thing about the imprisonment is the fact that it is caused by desire, so that the prisoner is the chief assistant in his own imprisonment.

"The lovers of learning, then, I say, know that philosophy, taking possession of the soul when it is in this state, encourages it gently and tries to set it free, pointing out that the eyes and the ears and the other senses are full of deceit. Philosophy urges the soul to withdraw from these, except insofar as their use is necessary, and exhorts it to collect and concentrate itself within itself, and to trust nothing except itself and its own abstract thought of abstract existence. And philosophy urges the soul to believe that there is no truth in that which it sees by other means and which varies with the various objects in which it appears, since everything of that kind is visible and apprehended by the senses, whereas the soul itself sees that which is invisible and apprehended by the mind.

"Now the soul of the true philosopher thinks that it must not resist this deliverance. Consequently, so far as the soul is able, it abstains from pleasures and desires and removes itself from griefs and fears, considering that whenever anyone experiences pleasure in excess, or violently fears or grieves or desires, he suffers evil from them—though not merely in the manner one might imagine, as with, for example, sickness or the expenditures incurred thanks to the desires. Rather, he suffers the greatest and most extreme evil and does not take it into account."[9]

The problem is that the body is unruly. Therefore, it requires discipline. Here's what Basil says: "On the contrary, we should discipline the body and hold it in check, even as we do the violent attacks of an untamed animal. We should quiet the restlessness and confusion produced by the body

*in the soul with the lash of reason, not giving full rein to pleasure. We
should do this instead of relaxing the reins and allowing the mind to be
swept along like a charioteer carried on by unmanageable and willful
horses.*"[10] *Once again, though not a precise match, his language echoes
Plato—in this case the way Plato (through Socrates) discusses the need to
discipline part of the soul in the* Phaedrus.

Socrates speaking "IN THE BEGINNING of this story I divided each soul
into three parts, two of which had the form of horses, the third that of
a charioteer. Let us keep this division. Now, of the horses, we said that
one is good and the other is not. But we did not fully say what the
virtue of the good is—nor the vice of the bad. That we must now do.

"The horse that stands at the right hand is upright and has clean
limbs. He carries his neck high, has an aquiline nose, is white in appearance, and has dark eyes. He is a lover of honor joined with moderation and self-respect, and a companion of true glory. He needs no
whip but is guided only by the word of command and by reason. The
other horse, however, is crooked, heavy, poorly put together—his
neck is short and thick, his nose flat, his color dark, his eyes grey and
bloodshot. He is the comrade of insolence and boastfulness, is
shaggy-eared and deaf, hardly obedient to whip and goad.

"Now when the charioteer beholds the love-inspiring vision,
and his whole soul is warmed by the sensation and is full of the
tickling of yearning, the horse that is obedient to the charioteer, con-
strained then as always by shame and self-respect, controls himself
and does not leap upon the beloved. But the other no longer obeys
the driving of the goad or whip of the charioteer, but violently
springs forward, causing all possible trouble to his yoke-mate and
to the charioteer. He forces them to approach the beloved and pro-
pose the joys of love. At first they strain back, angrily counteracting
the bad horse. They will not be forced to do terrible and unlawful
things. But finally, as the trouble has no end, they go forward with
him, yielding and agreeing to do his bidding.

"And they come to the beloved and behold his brilliant face.
And as the charioteer looks upon him, his memory is carried back
to the nature of beauty. And he sees beauty itself standing along

with moderation upon a pure and holy pedestal. And when he sees this he is afraid and falls backward, awe-stricken. And in falling he is forced to pull the reins so violently backward as to bring both horses upon their haunches. The one is quite willing since he does not oppose him, but the insolent one is very unwilling.

"And as they go away, one horse in his shame and astonishment soaks the whole soul with sweat. But the other, as soon as he is recovered from the pain of the bit and the fall, attempting to breathe, breaks into angry reproaches, bitterly abusing his yoke-mate and the charioteer for their cowardice and lack of manhood in deserting their post and breaking their agreement. And again, in spite of their unwillingness, he urges them forward and hardly yields to their request that he postpone the matter to another time.

"Then when the time comes that they have agreed on, they pretend that they have forgotten it, but he reminds them. And so, struggling and neighing and pulling, he forces them again with the same purpose to approach the beloved one. And when they are near him, he lowers his head, raises his tail, takes the bit in his teeth, and pulls shamelessly.

"The effect on the charioteer is the same as before but more pronounced. He falls back like a racer from the starting-rope, pulls the bit backward even more forcefully than before from the teeth of the insolent horse, covers his abusive tongue and jaws with blood, and forces his legs and haunches to the ground, causing him much pain.

"Now when the good-for-nothing horse has suffered the same experience many times, his insolence coming to an end, he is humbled and now follows the foresight and direction of the charioteer. And so, whenever he sees the beautiful one, he is overcome with fear. Consequently, from now on the soul of the lover meets the beloved with both shame and dread."[11]

Ultimately, the body should be oriented to the soul. Basil states that "We should attach ourselves to the body only insofar as we receive support from it in the pursuit of wisdom." He follows up the point by observing, "This is as Plato declares, speaking in a manner similar to Paul, who exhorts us to make no provision for the body as a location to satisfy the desires."[12]

Saint Paul's counsel is from the Letter to the Romans, in which he admonishes, "Clothe yourselves with the Lord Jesus Christ and do not think about how to satisfy the desires of the flesh."[13] *As for Plato, scholars have suggested that his comes from the* Republic *— as follows.*

Socrates speaking "While they are young boys and children, they should occupy themselves with an education and practice a philosophy that is suitable to their youthful age. And while they are growing up toward manhood, they should take very good care of their bodies in order to acquire assistants in their pursuit of philosophy. And with the advance of age, when the soul begins to reach maturity, they should increase the intensity of these exercises."[14]

Finally, Basil advises us to pursue real things rather than "shadows and dreams" — the good of the future life with God rather than present goods. "All of the goods of this present life together are far removed in worth from the smallest goods of the future life, even as shadows and dreams fall short of reality." [15] *We are helped in this pursuit by means of a training obtained from non-Christian Greek literature. Even so, Basil recognizes that this literature is like a "shadow and reflection" when compared to the literature of revelation. "Once we are ready, we will listen to the ineffable mysteries taught in the sacred writings. And like those who have become accustomed to seeing the reflection of the sun in the water, we will then direct our eyes to the light."* [16] *The imagery comes from Plato's famous allegory of the cave found in the* Republic.

Socrates speaking "NEXT," I SAID, "imagine our nature when it is educated and when it is not educated in terms of the following comparison. Picture human beings dwelling in a kind of subterranean cavern with a long entrance open to the light along its entire width. There they are, imprisoned from childhood, their legs and necks shackled so that they remain in the same spot, able only to look forward, and prevented by the shackles from turning their heads. Picture further the light from a fire burning higher up and at a distance behind them. And between the fire and the prisoners there is a pathway along which a low wall has been built, as the exhibitors of puppet-shows have partitions in front of the men themselves, above which they show the puppets."

"I see it," Glaucon said.

"See also, then, humans alongside the wall carrying things of all kinds that rise above the top of wall. They carry statues of men as well as other animals made of stone and wood and everything else. Some of these moving along carrying things are probably speaking, while some are silent."

"A strange image you speak of," he said, "and strange prisoners."

"It is like us," I said. "For, to begin with, tell me, do you think these men would have seen anything of themselves or of one another except the shadows cast from the fire on the wall of the cave that was in front of them?"

"How could they," he said, "if they were compelled to hold their heads unmoved through life?"

"And what about the things carried alongside the wall? Would not the same be true?"

"Without question."

"So then, if they were able to talk to one another, do you not think they would suppose that in naming the things they saw they were naming the passing objects?"

"Necessarily."

"And what if their prison had an echo from the wall in front of them? When one of those carrying things above uttered a sound, do you suppose the prisoners would think anything else than that the shadow going by was the speaker?"

"By Zeus, I do not," he said.

"Then in every way such prisoners would consider true reality to be nothing other than the shadows of the manmade objects."

"Quite necessarily," he said.

"Consider, then, what would be the manner of the release from these shackles and the healing from this folly if in the course of nature something of this sort should happen to them? That is, when one was released and compelled to stand up suddenly and turn his head around and walk and lift up his eyes to the light. And in doing all this he felt pain and, because of the dazzle and gleaming of the light, he was unable to see distinctly the objects whose shadows he formerly saw. What do you suppose his answer would be if someone told him that what he had seen before was all nonsense, but that now, being nearer to reality and turned toward things that are more real, he saw more truly? And also if one pointed out to him each of the passing objects and compelled him by questions to identify each one. Do you not think that he would be at a loss, and that he would regard what he formerly saw as truer than the things now pointed out to him?"

"Far more actual," he said.

"And if he were compelled to look at the light itself, would that not pain his eyes, and would he not turn away and flee to those things that he is able to see distinctly and judge them as in fact more clear and exact than the objects pointed out?"

"That's how it would be," he said.

"Yet if," I went on, "from there someone dragged him by force along the rough and steep way up, and if he did not let him go before he had dragged him out into the light of the sun, do you not think that he would find it painful and displeasing to be dragged along, and when he came out into the light, that his eyes would be filled with its rays so that he would not be able to see even one of the things that we call real or true?"

"No, not immediately," he said.

"Then there would be need of habituation, I suppose, to enable him to see the things farther up. And at first he would most easily see the shadows distinctly. After that, the images or reflections of men and other things in water. Still later, the things themselves. Beyond these, he would go on to gaze at things in the sky and at the sky itself. Looking at the light of the stars and the moon would be easier at night than looking at the sun and the light of the sun during the day."

"Of course."

"And so, finally, I suppose, he would see the sun—not its image in water or in some other place. But he would be able to gaze at the sun and look upon it by itself, in its own place, just as it is."

"Necessarily," he said.

"And at this point he would conclude that it is the sun that produces the seasons and the yearly cycles, and governs all things in the visible region, and is in some way the cause of all these things they had seen."

"Clearly," he said, "that would be the next thing to come."

"What then? What if he remembered his first dwelling place, and what passed for wisdom there, and those who were then his fellow-prisoners? Do you not think he would call himself happy for the change he's undergone and have pity on them?"

"Very much." . . .

"This image then, dear Glaucon, we must apply as a whole to all that has been said, comparing the region appearing through sight to the dwelling place of the prison, and the light of the fire in it to the power of the sun. And if you reckon that the passage up and the contemplation of the things above is the soul's ascent to the intelligible region, you will not miss my expectation, since that is what you desire to hear."[17]

HESIOD

One way to get knowledge is by learning a little at a time. Basil suggests that "the poet's saying about 'adding little to little' is true not only for the accumulation of money but also for gathering together every kind of knowledge."[18] The poet referenced is Hesiod; the poem is his Works and Days.

THE MAN WHO adds to what he has will ward off burning hunger. If you add only a little to a little, and you do this often, soon the "only a little" will become a lot. . . . If your spirit within you longs for wealth, then work in this way, and add work upon work.[19]

Having explained to his brother, Perses, the value of receiving counsel, Hesiod goes on to give advice about when and how to work throughout the year. Similarly, Basil remarks that if his students accept his advice they "will belong to the second category of men praised by Hesiod."[20] The passage once again comes from Hesiod's Works and Days.

BEST OF ALL is the man who thinks about everything himself, pondering how things will turn out in the end and what will be better. And noble too is the kind of man who is won over by good advice. But good for nothing is the man who doesn't think for himself or take to heart what he hears from another man. He's useless.[21]

What is the point about which Basil's readers should listen and receive advice? In Basil's mind, it is all about the good life, that of virtue. "It seems to me," he says, "that Hesiod had no other purpose in making these points than to turn us toward virtue and summon all men to be good."[22] Hesiod's Works and Days *is largely about how to do well—how to work hard and obtain success. Accordingly, Hesiod describes two paths. One path leads to success or excellence (aretē); the other leads to failure and misery (kakotēs).*

IT'S EASY TO grab at Failure (Kakotēs). It is there in abundance for you. The way is smooth to her, and she dwells very near to you. But the immortal gods have put sweat in front of Success (Aretē). The path to her is long and steep. And so it is rough-going at first. Nevertheless, when one comes to the highest point, then the path becomes easy—however hard it is *at first.*[23]

Basil goes on to say, "If any other man has celebrated virtue in the manner of Hesiod, let us favorably receive his words as leading to the same goal as our own."[24] In the final analysis, the Works and Days *is a lengthy admonishment and instruction manual about how to be happy. Here's what may be called Hesiod's happiness formula:*

DIVINELY FAVORED AND happy in wealth is the man who knows all these things and does his work, blameless before the immortals, distinguishing the birds of omen and shunning transgressions.[25]

XENOPHON

Basil relates a story about Heracles' encounter with Virtue and Vice personified, which is most notably found in Xenophon's Memorabilia. *Here's the beginning of Basil's account: "Furthermore, Prodicus, the sophist from Ceos, explored similar notions regarding virtue and vice in his own writings. Therefore, we must also apply our minds to him, not tossing the man out as worthless. Prodicus' account goes something like the following . . . When Heracles was quite young, just about your age right now, he was considering which road he should take—the one leading through suffering and toil to virtue or the easiest road. Just then, two women approached. These were Virtue and Vice."* [26]

The following is Xenophon's version. In it Socrates is speaking to the Cyrenaic philosopher Aristippus. For the sake of brevity, some of the passage is summarized in italics.

"THE WISE MAN Prodicus makes the same point regarding virtue in his tale about Heracles. When Heracles was making his way from boyhood to young manhood, and so he was on the path to becoming his own master, he came to the point where he had to choose between a life of virtue or one of vice. So he went out to a quiet spot and sat there puzzling over which path he should take.

"Sitting there, two very tall women appeared and walked up to him. One was fitting and noble in appearance—her body ordered with purity, her eyes adorned with modesty, and her bearing generally expressing discretion. She wore a white robe. But the other! She was plump and soft, with an unnatural pink and white face all made up, and an upright spine to exaggerate her height, and eyes wide open. As for her robe, it hung so as to reveal everything—all her charms. She eyed herself and looked away to see if anyone noticed her. She would also glance at her own shadow.

Socrates explains that it is these two women who approach Heracles, each making their case to him. The latter woman speaks first. Heracles should be her friend, she urges—if, that is, he wants to follow along the easiest and pleasantest road. He'll have the best of everything—food, drink, sex, sleep, scents, and every other pleasure. All sweets! No hardship! No war or worries! And no toil because he'll simply seize what he wants from others.

So then, Socrates said, when Heracles had heard her claims, he asked, "Lady, what is your name?" She responded, "My friends call me Happiness, but those who hate me have nicknamed me Vice."

Now the other woman speaks. She promises a good result if Heracles will only follow her path. Yet, she says, it won't be easy. "Of all that is truly good or noble, the gods give nothing to men without toil and effort."

This woman goes on to explain what a man must do to get various goods. Favor from the gods requires worship. Goodwill from friends calls for kindness. A city's honor demands service. Greek admiration—the hard work of excellence. Fruits require cultivation; an increase in flock numbers, shepherding; and defense and power, training in the art of war. Lastly, a strong body demands the mind's command and much toilsome, sweaty training.

Socrates went on, saying, "As Prodicus tells it, Vice here interrupted and said, 'Have you considered, Heracles, how long and hard this road to enjoyment is that this woman Virtue is mapping for you? I will lead you along a short and easy road to happiness.'"

Virtue strongly disagrees and declares, "But I associate with the gods and with good men, and no fine action, whether the deed of a god or of a man, is done without me. . . . So Heracles, child of good parents, if you toil hard along the path that I, Virtue, have mapped for you, you can acquire the most blessed happiness."

Finishing Prodicus' story, Socrates said, "Anyhow, Aristippus, you would do well to think about these matters and consider the life ahead of you."[27]

HOMER

Relying on the scholarship of others, Basil looks favorably upon Homer. "Now, as I myself have heard a man say who is skillful at closely examining the mind and meaning of a poet, all Homer's poetry is a commendation of virtue. And with Homer, everything apart from what is incidental leads to this end."[28] *To illustrate, Basil cites the episode in Homer's* Odyssey *when, after passing through a great deal of suffering and struggle, and nearly dying, Odysseus finally arrives on the Phaeacian island of Scheria. There he encounters the beautiful princess Nausicaa and eventually the rest of the Phaeacian nobility. Their response to him is ultimately one of*

amazement. Here's the passage at length (as before, the italic lines are sum-
maries).

BUT WHEN NAUSICAA thought about turning toward home once
again, and so about yoking the mules and folding up the beautiful
clothes, then did the goddess, bright-eyed Athena, form a new plan.
She would wake up Odysseus and have him see the sweet looking
girl. Then she would lead him to the city of the Phaeacian men.

Just then the princess threw the ball to one of the handmaidens.
But she missed her and instead threw it into a deep eddy. Seeing it
fall, they shouted aloud!

At this, godlike Odysseus awoke, sat up, and considered anx-
iously in his mind and spirit, "Ah me! To what land of mortals have
I come? Are they violent and insolent men? Are they uncivilized
and wild, without justice or the proper observance of custom? Or
are they hospitable men, loving strangers? And do they themselves
fear the gods in their minds?"

Odysseus thinks the voices may be those of nymphs. Not knowing, he
ventures from his resting place to look, breaking off a leafy branch to cover
his bare genitals. When they see him, the handmaidens flee. Not Nausicaa,
though. Despite his befouled looks, she stands opposite him with a courage
supplied by Athena. Meanwhile, Odysseus wonders whether he should ap-
proach her and take her knees as a suppliant or stand apart and call out to
her to give him clothing and show him the way to her city. Finally, he speaks.

"I take your knees, O queen. Are you a goddess or a mortal? If
you are a goddess, one of the gods who possess the wide sky above,
then I say that you are most like Artemis, the daughter of mighty
Zeus, in your looks, form, and stature. But if you are a mortal living
on the earth, then three times blessed are your father and queen
mother, and three times blessed are your brothers, too. Surely their
spirits forever grow warm with happy thoughts because of you,
seeing such a beautiful flower entering the dance. But that one is
blessed in his heart above all others who prevails with wedding
gifts and leads you home. For with my own eyes, I've never seen a
mortal such as you are—whether a man or a woman. Awe holds
me as I look at you."

Odysseus compares Nausicaa to a young tree he once saw on Apollo's altar in Delos. He goes on to explain his trouble from afar.

"Sorrow that is hard to bear has come upon me. Yesterday, on the twentieth day, I escaped from the wine-faced sea. During all that time, waves and rushing wind carried me away from the island of Ogygia. And now some god has tossed me ashore here so that I may yet surely suffer even more evil. My guess is that the misfortune won't stop yet—not until the gods give me more.

"But pity me, O queen. I have come upon you first after much suffering and toil, and I know nothing about the men who hold the land here or the city. Show me to the city, and give me some rag to throw around myself, perhaps the cloth you used to carry the clothing when you came here. And may the gods grant you as much as your heart eagerly desires—a man for a husband, and a house. And may that noble unity of mind and feeling accompany these. For nothing is greater and nothing better than when a man and woman dwell in their household with the same thoughts, feelings, and mind—a huge pain to their enemies and joy to their friends. Their glory is very well known."

In reply, white-armed Nausicaa said, "Stranger, since you do not seem to be a base or senseless man, and since Olympian Zeus himself dispenses fortune and happiness to men, to both the good and the bad as he wills, whether he be brave or a coward, noble or base—so I believe that surely he has given misfortune to you. Regardless, you must endure it either way. But now, since you have come to our land and city, you will have whatever any suppliant who has suffered much would need—clothing or anything. I will show you to the city, and I will tell you the name of the people. The Phaeacians hold this land and city, and I am the daughter of greathearted Alcinous, who holds power and strength from the Phaeacians."

Seeing that her handmaidens are running off for fear of Odysseus, Nausicaa attempts to calm them, assuring them that the distance of Scheria and the care of the gods will defend them against all harm. But more, they have a duty to help him.

"But this man who has come here is some unhappy wanderer. And now we must take care of him since all strangers and beggars come from Zeus—and a gift, even if small, is valued. So my hand-maidens, give the stranger food and drink, and wash him in the river in a spot sheltered from the wind."

Nausicaa's handmaidens obey. But instead of bathing him in the river, Odysseus asks to bathe alone since he is so filthy. He does. And afterwards, Athena makes him appear taller, stronger, and handsomer than he earlier appeared. When Nausicaa finally gazes at him in awe, she says he is like one of the gods, and she wishes that he might stay and become her husband.

The maiden marveled at him. . . . "Not without the will of all the gods who hold Olympus does this man come among the godlike Phaeacians. Before he seemed shameful to me. Now he is like the gods!" . . .

Much later, after Odysseus makes his way to the house of Alcinous, the king and Nausicaa's father, Alcinous says, "Listen to me, you chief men and rulers of the Phaeacians. This stranger seems wise—to really know what he thinks and what he's talking about. But come. Let's give him a guest-gift, the kind that's fitting for a host to give."

Still later, the Phaeacian queen Arete (Alcinous' wife and Nausicaa's mother) praises Odysseus for his mind and looks and suggests that the Phaeacian nobility should give him more gifts. Her judgment is the same as her husband's, who declares that Odysseus has a "noble heart." When Homer finally describes Odysseus' voyage home in a Phaeacian ship, he affirms that the ship "carried a man that resembled the gods in counsel." [29]

Elsewhere Basil references Odysseus to demonstrate how a reader should deal with potentially harmful material, namely, "the words and deeds of wicked men." Readers should imitate Odysseus who did what it takes to avoid "the songs of the Sirens." [30] What follows is the account from Homer. The first part presents the enchantress Circe explaining to Odysseus what will happen when he encounters the Sirens and what he should do. The second part offers Odysseus' account of what happened. As before, the italic lines are summaries.

Circe speaking (through Odysseus' narration) "'YOU WILL FIRST reach the Sirens, who cast a spell on every man that comes to them. Whoever draws near to them in ignorance of this spell and hears the Sirens' clear singing, his wife and little children will never stand by his side, glad at his homecoming. Instead, the Sirens will enchant him with their sweet-sounding song. They are situated in a grassy meadow. Surrounding them is a huge pile of bones and rotting men, and on the bones the mushy skin is wasting away. Therefore, you should row past the Sirens and plug your comrades' ears with sweet beeswax that you have worked and pressed until it is soft so that none of them may hear. But if you yourself wish to hear them, then let them tie you up in the swift ship by your hands and your feet, so that you're upright against the mast, with the rope winding around you and the mast itself. That way you'll be able to enjoy listening to the two Sirens. But if you implore your comrades and call on them to set you free, then let them tie you with even more rope.'"

Thanks to the steady breeze sent by Circe, the well-built ship quickly reaches the island of the Sirens. Then, just as it comes into view, the wind stops and the waves grow still. Consequently, they lower the sail and row. Meanwhile, Odysseus prepares the wax, with the help of the sun's heat, and plugs his comrades' ears. In turn, they tie him securely to the mast. Soon, the Sirens spot them nearing the island, coming as close as the distance one man can shout to another and still make out what he's saying, and they begin to sing.

"'Come here as you go, much-praised Odysseus, great glory of the Achaeans. Steer your ship landward so that you may hear our singing voices. Up to now, no man has rowed his black ship past this island until he has listened to the sweet singing voices streaming from our mouths. Instead, he takes pleasure in hearing us and goes away knowing more—for we know everything that happened throughout wide Troy. We know all the pain that the Argives and Trojans suffered because of the desire and will of the gods. Truly, we know whatever happens upon the much-nourishing earth.'

Odysseus speaking "That's what the Sirens said, letting their beautiful voices flow. My heart longed to listen, and so I directed my comrades to untie me with the nod of my head and brows—but they fell to their oars and rowed on. And at once Perimedes and Eurylochus stood up and tied me with even more ropes and drew them even tighter.

"But when they had rowed past the island—far enough so that we could no longer hear their clear voices or their song—then my faithful comrades took out the beeswax I had put in their ears, and they set me free from my bonds."[31]

The following texts present various notions that appear in both Basil's work and in Greek literature.

In reference to the man who says one thing but thinks another (the example comes from Euripides' tragedy the Hippolytus*), Basil judges, "Such a man seeks the appearance of being good rather than actually being good. Even so, this is the height of injustice—if we must obey the words of Plato, which forbid the appearance of being just without actually being so."* [32] *As the following brief passages indicate, the general idea is common among ancient writers. The point is integrity—that one should be good rather than merely appear good.*

AESCHYLUS: *About the hero Amphiaraus, who has a simple shield, a scout reports:* "No symbol was fixed to his shield's circle. For he does not wish to appear the bravest, but to be the bravest."[33]

PLATO: "The height of injustice is to seem just without being so." *And,* "A man should study not to seem to be good but to be good, whether in private or in public life."[34]

DIOGENES LAERTIUS (*Referring to Diogenes of Sinope, the Cynic*): "He would generally chide men for the way they prayed, declaring that they asked for the seemingly good rather than the truly good."[35]

EPICURUS: "We must not merely pretend to practice philosophy; rather, we must actually do it. For we do not merely need the appearance of health, but true health."[36]

CICERO: (*Laelius speaking*) "It is not virtue I am talking about but a reputation for virtue. For many wish not so much to be, as to seem to be, endowed with real virtue. Such men delight in flattery, and when a complimentary speech is fashioned to suit their fancy, they think the empty phrase is proof of their own merits."[37]

SALLUST: "Cato's ambition was that of moderation, discretion, and, above all, austerity. He did not contend in splendor with the rich, or in faction with the seditious, but with the brave in fortitude, with the modest in simplicity, with the temperate in abstinence. He was more desirous to be, than to appear, virtuous."[38]

GREGORY OF NAZIANZUS: *Of Basil the Great, Gregory reports,* "His aim was ever to be, not to seem, most excellent."[39]

Another notion dear to Basil is that one seeking the good life should limit himself to "needs." Such "need" is the measure of satisfaction rather than pleasure or any other desire that surpasses need. As Basil declares, "Such a man will scorn that which surpasses need—even if it is the gold dust of Lydia or the product of the gold gathering ants. As his need for the thing decreases, his scorn for its excessive use will increase. And doubtlessly he will define 'need' itself in terms of the necessary requirements of nature, and not in terms of pleasure. Those who go beyond the bounds of necessity resemble people who rush headlong down a slope. They are unable to grab hold of anything to stop their precipitous fall. No, the more they grasp at things, the more things they need to satisfy the desires." [40] *The idea echoes the passage in Plato's* Republic *where Socrates, Adeimantus, and Glaucon seek in thought and words to build a city in order to discover the true nature of justice. They soon observe their city of need, the healthy city, morphing into a city of luxury, a diseased city. As before, the italic lines are summaries.*

Socrates "COME, THEN, LET us create a city from the beginning, in theory. Its real creator, as it appears, will be our needs."
   Adeimantus "Obviously."
   "Now the first and chief of our needs is the provision of food for existence and life."
   "Assuredly."
   "The second is housing, and the third is clothing and that sort of thing."

"That is so."

"Tell me, then," I said, "how our city will suffice for the provision of all these things. Will there not be a farmer for one, and a builder, and then again a weaver? And shall we add thereto a cobbler and some other purveyor for the needs of the body?"

"Certainly."

"The indispensable minimum of a city, then, would consist of four or five men."

"Apparently." . . .

After discussing the nature of each member of the city, and the work each contributes, and the fact that the city would further require other workers to make things and supply provisions for the original few, and that it would require imports and thus exports for trade, and so tradesmen and markets and shopkeepers—after discussing this, Socrates turns to describe what sort of city they have so far constructed.

"First of all, then, let us consider what will be the manner of life of men thus provided. Will they not make bread and wine and garments and shoes? And they will build themselves houses and carry on their work in summer for the most part unclad and unshod and in winter clothed and shod sufficiently? And for their nourishment they will provide meal from their barley and flour from their wheat, and kneading and cooking these they will serve noble cakes and loaves on some arrangement of reeds or clean leaves. And reclined on rustic beds strewn with bryony and myrtle, they will feast with their children, drinking of their wine thereto, garlanded and singing hymns to the gods in pleasant fellowship, not begetting offspring beyond their means for fear that they will fall into poverty or war?"

Here Glaucon broke in: "No relishes apparently," he said, "for the men you describe as feasting."

"True," I said. "I forgot that they will also have relishes—salt, of course, and olives and cheese and onions and greens, the sort of things they boil in the country, they will boil up together. But for dessert we will serve them figs and chickpeas and beans, and they will toast myrtle berries and acorns before the fire, washing them down with moderate drinks. And so, living in peace and health, they will probably die in old age and hand on a similar life to their offspring."

Glaucon furthermore said, "If you were founding a city of pigs, Socrates, what other fodder than this would you provide?"

"Why, what would you have, Glaucon?" I said.

"What is customary," he replied. "They must recline on couches, I presume, if they are not to be uncomfortable, and dine from tables and have made dishes and sweetmeats such as are now in use."

"Good," I said, "I understand. It is not merely the origin of a city, it seems, that we are considering, but the origin of a luxurious city. Perhaps that isn't such a bad suggestion, either. For by observation of such a city it may be we could discern the origin of justice and injustice in states. The true state I believe to be the one we have described—the healthy state, as it were. But if it is your pleasure that we contemplate also a fevered state, there is nothing to hinder. For there are some, it appears, who will not be contented with this sort of fare or with this way of life. But couches will have to be added thereto and tables and other furniture, yes, and relishes and myrrh and incense and girls and cakes—all sorts of all of them. And the requirements we first mentioned, houses and garments and shoes, will no longer be confined to necessities, but we must set painting to work and embroidery, and procure gold and ivory and similar adornments, must we not?"

"Yes," he said.

"Then we shall have to enlarge the city again. For that healthy state is no longer sufficient, but we must proceed to swell out its bulk and fill it up with a multitude of things that exceed the requirements of necessity in states, as, for example, the entire class of huntsmen, and the imitators, many of them occupied with figures and colors and many with music—the poets and their assistants, rhapsodists, actors, chorus dancers, and contractors—and the manufacturers of all kinds of articles, especially those that have to do with women's adornment. And so we shall also want more servers. Don't you think that we shall need tutors, nurses wet and dry, beauty shop ladies, barbers, and yet again cooks and chefs? And we will have need, further, of swineherds. There were none of these creatures in our former city, for we had no need of them, but in this city there will be this further need. And we will also require other cattle in great numbers if they are to be eaten, shall we not?"

"Yes."

"Doctors, too, are something whose services we will be much more likely to require if we live in this manner than as before?"

"Much."

"And the territory, I presume, that was then sufficient to feed the then population, from being adequate will become too small. Is that so or not?"

"It is."

"Then we shall have to cut out a portion of our neighbor's land if we are to have enough for pasture and plowing, and they in turn of ours if they too abandon themselves to the unlimited acquisition of wealth, disregarding the limit set by our necessary wants."

"Inevitably, Socrates."

"We will go to war as the next step, Glaucon—or what will happen?"

"What you say," he said.

"And we are not yet to speak," I said, "of any evil or good effect of war, but only to affirm that we have further discovered the origin of war, namely, from those things from which the greatest disasters, public and private, come to states when they come."[41]

"Certainly."

"Then, my friend, we must still further enlarge our city by no small increment, but by a whole army that will march out and fight it out with assailants in defense of all our wealth and the luxuries we have just described."[42]

Finally, there's what the philosopher Epicurus advised about which desires to satisfy and why. [43]

WE MUST CONSIDER that of the desires, some are natural, and some are groundless. Of the natural desires, some are necessary, and some are merely natural. And of the necessary desires, some are necessary for happiness, some for freeing the body from disturbance, and some for living itself.[44] *And,* We must obey nature rather than doing violence to her. We will obey nature by satisfying the necessary desires and the natural desires, too, as long as they do no harm, but sharply rejecting the harmful desires.[45]

According to Gregory of Nazianzus, Basil himself lived a simple life defined by basic needs rather than luxury.

WHAT DID HE possess besides his body and the necessary coverings of the flesh? His wealth was having nothing, and he thought the cross, with which he lived, more precious than great riches. . . . He was poor and unkempt, yet without ostentation. . . . A wondrous thing is moderation, and fewness of wants, and freedom from the dominion of pleasures, and from the bondage of that cruel and degrading mistress, the belly. Who was so independent of food, and, without exaggeration, more free from the flesh? For he flung away all satiety and surfeit to creatures destitute of reason, whose life is slavish and debasing. He paid little attention to such things as, next to the appetite, are of equal rank, but, as far as possible, lived on the merest necessaries, his only luxury being to prove himself not luxurious.[46]

Finally, there is the benefit of examples. For Basil, one benefit of non-Christian literature is its presentation of examples upon which we may model our own lives. We find the same emphasis in the Roman historian Livy, who writes:

WHAT CHIEFLY MAKES the study of history wholesome and profitable is this, that you behold the lessons of every kind of experience set out as on a conspicuous monument. From these you may choose for yourself and for your own state what examples to imitate. You may also choose what examples to avoid imitating—what is shameful from beginning to end.[47]

Similarly, the Greek historian Polybius began his history by noting:

HAD THE PRAISE of history been passed over by former chroniclers it would perhaps have been incumbent upon me to urge the choice and special study of records of this sort, as the readiest means men can have of correcting their knowledge of the past. But my predecessors have not been sparing in this respect. They have all begun and ended, so to speak, by enlarging on this theme: asserting again and again that the study of history is in the truest sense an education and a training for political life; and that the most instructive, or, rather, the only method of learning to bear with dignity the vicissitudes of fortune is to recall the catastrophes of others.[48]

Then there is the declaration of the historian Diodorus Siculus.

TO RECOUNT THE lives of men of the past is a task that presents difficulties to writers, and yet it is of no little profit to society as a whole. For such an account that clearly portrays in all frankness their base as well as their noble deeds renders honor to the good and abases the wicked by means of the censures as well as the praises that appropriately come to each group. The praise constitutes, one might say, a reward for excellence. . . . It is a noble thing for later generations to bear in mind, that whatever manner of life a man chooses to live while on this earth, such will be the remembrance that he will be thought worthy to have after his death. This principle should be followed so that later generations may not set their hearts upon the erection of memorials in stone that are limited to a single spot and subject to quick decay, but upon reason and the excellences in general.

Time, which withers all else, preserves for these excellences an immortality. . . .

Throughout our entire treatise . . . we have justly praised good men for their noble deeds and criticized base men whenever they have missed the mark. We believe that, by this means, we will lead men whose nature fortunately inclines them to excellence to undertake, because of the immortality fame and reputation accords them, the noblest deeds, whereas by appropriate criticism we will turn men of the opposite character from their impulse to vice.[49]

NOTES

[1] Basil, *How to Benefit from Reading Greek Literature* 3.3-4.
[2] Acts 7.22.
[3] Exodus 3.14.

[4] Daniel 1.4.

[5] Basil, *How to Benefit from Reading Greek Literature* 9.1.

[6] Plato, *Apology* 29d-30a.

[7] Basil, *How to Benefit from Reading Greek Literature* 9.2.

[8] Plato, *Phaedo* 64c-65a.

[9] Ibid., 82d-83c.

[10] Basil, *How to Benefit from Reading Greek Literature* 9.14.

[11] Plato, *Phaedrus* 253c-254e.

[12] Basil, *How to Benefit from Reading Greek Literature* 9.12.

[13] Romans 13.14.

[14] Plato, *Republic* 6.498b-c.

[15] Basil, *How to Benefit from Reading Greek Literature* 2.4.

[16] Ibid., 2.6 and 8.

[17] Plato, *Republic* 7.514a-516c; 517a-b.

[18] Basil, *How to Benefit from Reading Greek Literature* 10.2.

[19] Hesiod, *Works and Days* 361-363; 381-382.

[20] Basil, *How to Benefit from Reading Greek Literature* 1.3.

[21] Hesiod, *Works and Days* 293-297.

[22] Basil, *How to Benefit from Reading Greek Literature* 5.5.

[23] Hesiod, *Works and Days* 286-292. For Hesiod, *kakotēs* connotes failure in terms of mediocrity, inferiority, badness, harm, misery, and misfortune. "Badness" does not imply moral evil or vice as the later Greek tradition and others, including Basil, come to understand it. Rather, as in Homer, badness is failure, the inability to survive and thrive. By contrast, *aretē* connotes success in terms of excellence, superiority, goodness, benefit, thriving, and prosperity. Just as with "badness," "goodness" does not imply moral goodness or virtue; rather, it is success, the ability to survive and thrive to the greatest extent possible.

[24] Basil, *How to Benefit from Reading Greek Literature* 5.5.

[25] Hesiod, *Works and Days* 826-828.

[26] Basil, *How to Benefit from Reading Greek Literature* 5.11-12.

[27] Xenophon, *Memorabilia* 2.1-34. Note, by the way, the similarity to Hesiod's account of the two roads leading to Success (Virtue) and Failure (Vice). Doubtlessly, Prodicus (and Xenophon) had Hesiod in mind when telling the story of Heracles. For another account of the same story, see Philostratus the Athenian, *Life of Apollonius* 6.10.

[28] Basil, *How to Benefit from Reading Greek Literature* 5.6. N.G. Wilson concludes that, in his claim about Homer and virtue, Basil was likely referencing Horace (first century BC) or Dio Chrysostom (first century AD). We see, for instance, a strong admiration for the moral side of Homer's poems in Horace's second epistle. There he explains to the Roman politician Lollius that he has been going over

the "writer of the Trojan War [Homer], who teaches more clearly, and better than Chrysippus and Crantor, what is honorable, what is shameful, what is profitable, and what is not so." As for Dio Chrysostom, he asserts in one discourse that "since everything Homer wrote is both beneficial and useful, it would be a vast undertaking to go through everything he has said about virtue and vice" (53.11). In another discourse comparing Homer and Socrates, Dio explains that "both were devoted to and spoke about the same things . . . human virtue and vice, and things done poorly and things done well, and truth and deceit, and how the many have only opinions while the wise have true knowledge" (55.9). Finally, he cites Alexander the Great's view of Homer with approbation, that "Homer is a marvelous and truly divine herald of virtue" (2.41).

[29] Homer, *Odyssey* 6.115-243; 8.387-389; 11.335-341; 13.89.

[30] Basil, *How to Benefit from Reading Greek Literature* 4.2.

[31] Homer, *Odyssey* 12.35-54; 166-200.

[32] Basil, *How to Benefit from Reading Greek Literature* 6.5.

[33] Aeschylus, *Seven against Thebes* 591-592.

[34] Plato, *Republic* 2.361a and *Gorgias* 527b.

[35] Diogenes Laertius, *Lives and Opinions of Eminent Philosophers* 6.42. For an extended discourse on the topic, see Teles the Cynic's first discourse, "On Appearing and Being."

[36] Epicurus, *Vatican Saying* 54.

[37] Cicero, *On Friendship* 98.

[38] Sallust, *Conspiracy of Catiline* 54.

[39] Gregory of Nazianzus, *Oration* 43.60.

[40] Basil, *How to Benefit from Reading Greek Literature* 9.18-19.

[41] Plato may have had Odysseus' observation in mind: "There is no hiding a hungry belly. It is an accursed, destructive thing, which introduces many evils to all men. It is because of hunger that well-benched ships are made ready to sail the barren sea and carry misery and sorrow to hostile men" (Homer, *Odyssey* 17.285-289).

[42] Plato, *Republic* 2.369c-374a (trans. Paul Shorey, modified).

[43] We should note that for various reasons, Basil would have never directly referred to Epicurus or his pleasure-centered philosophy. That admitted, the similarity is too great in this instance to resist citing Epicurus.

[44] Diogenes Laertius, *Lives and Opinions of Eminent Philosophers* (from Epicurus' *Letter to Menoeceus*) 10.127.

[45] Epicurus, *Vatican Sayings* 21.

[46] Gregory of Nazianzus, *Oration* 43.60-61.

[47] Titus Livius (Livy), *The History of Rome* 1.10.

[48] Polybius, *Histories* 1.2.

[49] Diodorus Siculus, *Library* 10.12.1-2; 15.1.1.

PART 3
Points of Wisdom & Ways of Practice

- Principles for Reading Literature
from Basil the Great

- Points of Wisdom from Basil the Great

- Ways of Practice Following Basil the Great

Principles for Reading Literature
From Basil the Great

The following advice presents what Basil the Great might have said if he had reduced his work, How to Benefit from Reading Greek Literature, *to a list of top ten principles for reading. His counsel also applies to other forms of media—music, movies, online material, and the like. The "you" simply represents the reader.*

1. **Read with advice.** Seek out and listen to the counsel of trusted and experienced readers for advice on what and how to read.

2. **Read with the help of reason and wisdom.** Realize that it is reason bolstered by wisdom that gives you the best guidance in reading rather than your feelings.

3. **Read with reserve and discrimination.** Know that not all you read is beneficial; therefore, do not always give yourself over to your reading.

4. **Read with a goal in mind.** Remember where you are going and how literature may (or may not) help you get there.

5. **Read for what is useful, beneficial.** Know the difference between what is beneficial and harmful or useful and useless, and that some literature is harmful and useless.

6. **Read keeping in mind what is truly valuable.** Explore what matters and make that the center of your life. Excellent (virtuous) men and women are the best indicators of what is actually rather than seemingly valuable. When reading, keep these things in mind.

7. **Read to nourish your soul** (or mind). Care of the soul should be one of your central concerns when reading. You are what you read.

8. **Read in order to train.** Use literature as the means by which you practice to live a better life. Read hard. Train hard. Live well.

9. **Read for models.** Search your reading for examples of good men and women to imitate, those who are virtuous or excellent; simultaneously note the poor examples of those you should not imitate.

10. **Read in order to act.** Reading and the thoughts and feelings that originate with reading should always give rise to corresponding behavior—to achieve the good and avoid the bad.

POINTS OF WISDOM
FROM BASIL THE GREAT

The following points of wisdom, some slightly modified, come from Basil the Great's How to Benefit from reading Greek Literature. *Each point begins with a brief summary. For more points of wisdom organized by topic, read The Classics Cave's* The Wisdom & Way of Basil the Great.

Know what is useful My advice for you is that you should accept from the famous thoughts and words of ancient men only what is useful and know what to disregard. . . . You should not once and for all hand over the rudder of your mind to these men—as one might hand over the rudder of a ship to another—to follow along with them wherever they steer you. *Again,* you should accept from them only what is useful and know what to disregard.

Have a plan Consider: if a ship's captain does not randomly deliver his vessel over to the winds without a plan, but he steers the ship directly to port, or if an archer shoots at a target, or, also, if some bronzesmith or carpenter strives for the end proper to his craft, then what reason would there be for us to be less than such practitioners in terms of the ability to generally perceive our own interests?

Let your intellect be the guide If there were no intellect guiding our souls, then we would be like ships without ballast, carried everywhere and nowhere throughout life, without a plan or a purpose.

Let reason be your guide A prudent man . . . should make sound reason the guide of his life so that—even if he must speak against all other men and risk their contempt for the sake of what is noble—he will not at all shift away from that which he knows to be right.

Look for soul benefit We must associate with poets, prose writers, orators, and all other men . . . with whomever and wherever we may expect to find some benefit relative to the care of our souls.

Heed the words and deeds of good men; beware of bad men Whenever poets recount for you the words or deeds of good men, you should be pleased with them and admire them, earnestly trying to imitate such as these. Whenever poets go through the words and deeds of wicked men, you should avoid such imitation, stopping up your ears just as much as Odysseus did . . . when he avoided the songs of the Sirens.

You behave as you read Habitual contact with the bad words and deeds of *certain* writings is a road leading to bad behavior.

Be a critic; know what to praise We will not praise the poets when they portray people engaged in passionate love affairs or drinking to the point of intoxication. Nor when they define happiness in terms of tables brimming with food and depraved songs.

Let need correspond to nature The man who has been brought up to be free of *admiration for anything other men possess and the pleasures that come through the body* will not likely prefer anything base or shameful in word or deed. Such a man will scorn that which surpasses need. . . . He will define "need" itself in terms of the necessary requirements of nature, and not in terms of pleasure.

Guard your soul We must watch over our souls with every safeguard, so that we may not unknowingly accept something of the worse kind through the pleasure of the poets' words, like those who ingest poisons sweetened with honey.

Collect what is beneficial Those who make it their business to collect whatever is beneficial from every writing are like rivers that grow larger by taking in the flow of streams from every side. The poet *Hesiod's* saying about "adding little to little" is true not only for the accumulation of money but also for gathering together every kind of knowledge.

Read like a bee We should engage with literature in a way that follows the image of the bees. For bees neither approach nor land upon every flower without discrimination. Nor do they attempt to carry off the whole flower. Instead, taking only as much as is useful for their work, they are glad to give up the rest.

Gather soul benefit like a bee Just as bees know how to extract honey from flowers, which to men are enjoyable only for their sweet fragrance and color, even so with literature, those who look beyond the sweet and agreeable aspects of such writings may gather from them some benefit for their souls.

Read wisely If we are wise and moderate, we will acquire from literature whatever is suitable to us and akin to the truth, while passing over the rest.

Only accept what is useful We should not admit everything without discrimination; instead, we should only accept what is useful. For it is shameful to reject foods that are harmful yet to take no thought about the learning that nourishes the soul and, instead, to rush on like a mountain torrent, sweeping everything it happens upon.

Gather what is beneficial like a gardener Just as we avoid the thorns while picking flowers from a rose garden, let us guard against what is harmful when gathering whatever is useful from writings such as these.

Pay attention to virtue and vice in your reading; practice virtue We will certainly accept those passages *in literature* in which authors praise virtue and condemn vice. . . . It is through virtue that we must enter upon this life of ours. . . .Virtue is the only possession that cannot be taken away. . . . Virtue remains while we are living and when we have completed this life.

Choose the best life Let us remember the words of the man who urged everyone to choose the life that is in itself best, in the expectation that this life will become agreeable when we make a habit of it.

Associate with virtue Much has been said in celebration of virtue by the poets and prose writers, and even more by the philosophers. We must particularly turn our attention and apply ourselves to such literature. It is no small advantage for a certain friendliness and habitual association with virtue to be produced in the souls of the young.

Read Homer in light of virtue The interpreter of the poet's meaning said that Homer practically shouts it aloud in these passages, saying, "You must care for virtue, men—virtue, which swims ashore with the shipwrecked man and makes him, when he comes naked to dry land, more honored than the prosperous Phaeacians."

Travel the way of virtue The road that leads to virtue is more pleasant than the other road that leads to wickedness—which one may have in abundance from near at hand, as *Hesiod* says. Hesiod had no other purpose in making these points *about the roads to virtue and to wickedness* than to turn us toward virtue and summon all men to be good, and so that we might not become weak and cowardly when faced with suffering and toil, quitting before we reach the goal. If any other man has celebrated virtue in the manner of Hesiod, let us favorably receive his words as leading to the same goal as our own.

Take note of outstanding deeds As for the literature that contains counsel regarding noble conduct, let us receive it in this manner. And since the outstanding deeds of the men of old have also been preserved for us, either by means of an ongoing oral tradition or safeguarded in the words of the poets and prose writers, then let us not overlook this source in terms of benefit.

Observe the example of the philosopher Socrates of Athens A certain man kept striking Socrates, the son of Sophroniscus, in the face, attacking him without mercy. Even so, he did not oppose the man. Rather, he allowed the man, who was drunk with wine, to take his fill of anger, so that his face ended up swollen and bruised thanks to the blows. Now, when the man stopped striking him, Socrates, it is said, did nothing more than write on his forehead in the manner of a sculptor signing a sculpture, "So-and-so made this." So far did Socrates defend himself. . . . This example of Socrates is akin to that precept of ours which says that we should not defend ourselves against the man who strikes us on the cheek; rather, we should also offer the other cheek.

Know that you are training for a great contest We should see our lives in terms of athletic contests. . . . The competitors prepare themselves with practice exercises for the contests in which crowns are offered. . . . In short, the training prepares them for their contests.

Practice! Great is the power that is supplied by goal-oriented practice, both in terms of music and athletic competitions.

Observe the example of athletes in training Athletes endure countless hardships, and increase their strength by every possible means, and shed rivers of sweat while toiling in the gymnasium, and suffer many blows in the trainer's school, and choose not the tastiest food but that selected by the professional trainer, and so pass their days in every other way, so that before the contest their lives are a preparation and training for the contest. When the moment comes, *athletes* strip for the race and undergo every hardship and run every risk in order to win.

There is truth in the saying of Pittacus, that "It is hard to be good."

Observe the example of the hero Heracles When Heracles was quite young, just about your age right now, he was considering which road he should take—the one leading through suffering and toil to virtue or the easiest road. Just then, two women approached. These were Virtue and Vice. . . . Virtue promised nothing relaxed or pleasant. Instead, she offered him a whole ocean of sweat—countless sufferings and toils and dangers through every land and sea.

Know what is truly valuable Do not assume . . . that this human life of ours is altogether something valuable. Do not consider or call something entirely good which merely contributes to this life alone.

Care for your soul The soul is more valuable than the body in all things. What are we to do? . . . What else than to devote ourselves to the care of our souls, keeping all our leisure time free from other things. We should provide the soul with the best things.

Free your soul Through the wisdom of philosophy we should free the soul as though from a prison from its association with the passions of the body.

Purify your mind; know yourself Each one of us, whoever he is, requires extraordinary wisdom to recognize and know himself. Unless we have purified our minds, knowing ourselves is more impossible than it is for a man with darkened eyes to look up at the sun.

Scorn certain pleasures Purification of the soul includes scorning those pleasures that satisfy the senses.

As is necessary, take care of your body In all . . . matters *regarding the body*, we must be governed by necessity, only giving to the body as much as is beneficial to the soul.

Control your body We should discipline the body and hold it in check, even as we do the violent attacks of an untamed animal. We should quiet the restlessness and confusion produced by the body in the soul with the lash of reason, not giving full rein to pleasure. Do this instead of relaxing the reins and allowing the mind to be swept along like a charioteer carried on by unmanageable and willful horses. . . . Excessive care for the body is not only unprofitable for the body but also an impediment to the soul.

Much wealth is unnecessary If we make it our practice to look down on the body, taking no notice of it, we will hardly admire anything other men possess. After all, what use will we have for wealth if we scorn the pleasures that come through the body? As for me, I see no use—unless there is, as with the dragons found in legends, some pleasure in guarding hidden treasure!

WAYS OF PRACTICE
FOLLOWING BASIL THE GREAT

The following ways of practice, inspired by Basil the Great's How to Benefit from Reading Greek Literature, *are offered with the goal of practice in mind, the application of ancient wisdom to our contemporary ways and lives. We hope they will serve, in some small measure, as a source of inspiration and motivation. Use them to contemplate your life, where you are now, where you are going, and how you can better get there. For more, pick up The Classics Cave's* Basil the Great Workbook & Journal. *One last note. You will likely find that the space given for responses is not enough. If so, jot your thoughts and practices down in a separate place.*

PRACTICE 1: STEERING TO YOUR PORT & HITTING YOUR TARGETS

"Consider: if a ship's captain does not randomly deliver his vessel over to the winds without a plan, but he steers the ship directly to port, or if an archer shoots at a target . . . then what reason would there be for us to be less than such practitioners in terms of the ability to generally perceive our own interests?" —Basil the Great

My Interests • What are your "interests" in life? What is valuable to you? What are your targets?

_____

_____

_____

_____

_____

_____

_____

_____

Your life is a great journey. Do you know where you are sailing? Today? Tomorrow? Later?

My Present Location ▪ Where are you right now in your life?

_____

_____

_____

_____

_____

_____

My Ports ▪ To what ports are you sailing? What are your goals?

When considering the latter question, keep in mind the areas of your life that are important to you, areas for which you may want to determine goals (for example, goals related to your character; your soul—your innermost life; your education and career; your hobbies and other things you want to do; your life circumstances— where you live, how, etc.; your family and friends; and the like). You may also wish to consider your goals relative to the short-term, mid-term, and long-term.

_____

_____

_____

_____

_____

_____

_____

_____

My Plans • What is your plan?—to reach your ports, achieve your goals? For this month? This year? What is your plan of life?

_____

_____

_____

_____

My Winds • What are the "winds" that blow you off course? Do you ever "randomly *give yourself* over to the winds without a plan"?

_____

_____

_____

_____

PRACTICE 2: TAKING CONTROL OF MY MIND BY GUARDING MY MIND'S RUDDER AND BEING AWARE OF WHO IS STEERING

For Basil, our minds are like a ship that we must steer in one direction or another, to this or that port. Are we steering our ship or is someone else?

"My advice for you is that you should accept from the famous thoughts and words of ancient men only what is useful and know what to disregard. . . . You should not once and for all hand over the rudder of your mind to these men—as one might hand over the rudder of a ship to another—to follow along with them wherever they steer you." —Basil the Great

"A prudent man . . . should make sound reason the guide of his life."
—Basil the Great

I can either be steered by my own thoughts or those of others. If steered by others, I can welcome an influence that is beneficial and healthy or the opposite. This influence—ideas, views, suggestions, persuasions, attitudes, feelings, values, goals—comes from a variety of media, including "the famous thoughts and words of ancient men," as well as those who are influential today. Books. Blogs. Online forums. Apps. Social Media. Videos. Music. Podcasts. Advertisements. And so on.

Q • Who or what holds the rudder of my mind? What steers me?

_____

_____

_____

_____

Q • In what ways do different forms of media, including literature, steer me?

_____

_____

_____

_____

Resolution & Practice • How can I take (or retake) control of the rudder of my mind? What specific steps can I take to welcome "what is useful" or beneficial and "disregard" the rest?

_____

_____

_____

_____

_____

PRACTICE 3: COLLECTING THE BENEFICIAL

"Those who make it their business to collect whatever is beneficial from every writing are like rivers that grow larger by taking in the flow of streams from every side. The poet *Hesiod's* saying about 'adding little to little' is true not only for the accumulation of money but also for gathering together every kind of knowledge."

—Basil the Great

Add to your Benefit Collection Basket • Over the next week, collect five points of benefit from whatever media you use and add them to your Benefit Collection Basket. How does each benefit you?

▪ BENEFIT COLLECTION BASKET ▪

1. _____

_____

2. _____

_____

3. _____

_____

4. _____

_____

5. _____

_____

PRACTICE 4: IDENTIFYING & PRACTICING VIRTUE

"We will certainly accept those passages *in literature* in which authors praise virtue and condemn vice. . . . It is through virtue that we must enter upon this life of ours." —Basil the Great

Identify It • Generally defined, what is virtue? (The Greek is *aretē*.)

_____

_____

_____

Specify It • What are three virtues? Give an example of each.

_____

_____

_____

Practice It • Describe concrete, specific, realistic ways you can practice *one* of the three above virtues over the course of the next week.

_____

_____

_____

Keep It Up •After practicing for a week, determine how you can continue to practice the virtue. What about the other virtues? How can you practice each? Again, be concrete, specific, realistic.

_____

_____

_____

_____

OTHER MATTERS OF INTEREST
Related to Basil the Great

SUMMARY OF BASIL'S ADDRESS ON
HOW TO BENEFIT FROM READING GREEK LITERATURE

The following presents the "In Brief" summaries that appear before each chapter that summarize Basil's address on How to Benefit from Reading Greek Literature.

G IVEN HIS LIFE experience and his warm relationship with his students, Basil the Great opens by declaring his wish to give them direction in life by showing them how to benefit from reading ancient literature. His intention is to explain how they may maintain control of their own minds while determining what is useful and what is not.

Basil goes on to describe the great difference in value between this present life and the future life. It is similar to the vast difference between shadows and real things. Consequently, he urges his students to be oriented to and prepare themselves for the life to come. The sacred writings found in the Bible are the primary means by which they may do so. Nevertheless, for people who are too young to dive into the profound teachings of these writings—as Basil's students are, he contends—it is beneficial to prepare by other means, namely, by means of literature outside the sacred writings. Paying attention to the good found in this other literature, his students will then be able to turn to the sacred writings once they are older and ready.

Basil next turns to how Christian and non-Christian writings correspond to each other and what the role of each is in education. He settles upon the image of a tree with its fruit and leaves. Although the fruit is the proper excellence of a tree, the leaves nonetheless serve it in their own way and excellence. Similarly, both Christian truth and non-Christian wisdom are proper and useful to the soul. Basil offers the biblical Moses and Daniel as examples. Both men studied non-scriptural wisdom before turning to the divine truth of the sacred Scriptures.

Having established that one may do so, Basil pivots to explore how one may benefit from non-Christian literature. Whether reading poetry or prose, the key is to focus on that which praises virtue and to avoid that which glorifies vice. A reader may do this by imitating the bee, he suggests, which gathers what is useful from the flower while leaving alone what is merely pleasurable. One may also imitate a gardener, who successfully gathers roses while avoiding their thorns.

Basil advises the young to pay attention to those passages in poetry and other writing having to do with virtue. Given the responsive and formable nature of their minds, this point is particularly important for them. He goes on to mention and give examples from five Greek authors (Hesiod, Homer, Solon, Theognis, Prodicus), who praise virtue and call on men to travel along her road rather than that of vice. All stress the superiority and benefits of virtue as compared with vice, as well as any other object or experience typically valued by humans.

Then there is the whole issue of living with integrity. Basil stresses the value of lining up one's actions with what one says and thinks. One should not merely strive for the appearance of virtue but its reality.

Basil counsels his students to take into account and imitate the examples of noble conduct and outstanding deeds from the past. These examples may serve as models. Among the models on display are Pericles of Athens, Eucleides of Megara, the philosopher Socrates, Alexander the Great, and Cleinias, the disciple of Pythagoras. Basil asserts that these men exemplify a handful of Christian principles: turning the other cheek; enduring another man's anger with patience and wishing for his good; avoiding lust in one's heart; and refusing to swear an oath.

Basil returns to his original and primary point—that readers should only take in what is useful from literature rather than everything without discrimination. When reading, readers should always keep in mind the ultimate goal.

Among other examples, Basil suggests that readers should behave like a ship's captain guiding his ship into port, or a musician or an athlete preparing for a contest. He mentions the renowned musician Timotheus, and the athletes Polydamas and Milo. As for the latter, in order to take first prize an athlete keeps his mind on the goal of winning the contest by rigorously training, and by enduring many hardships and the harsh advice of his trainers. So too should the young and others attentively and actively keep their minds on the final prize that is beyond words. He also advises them to keep in mind the place of punishment and correction reserved for those who prefer wrongdoing.

Basil counsels that his students' major concern should be the care of their souls. For this reason they should work to free their souls from the passions and desires of the body. They may do this by scorning everything that surpasses necessity. He defines necessity, or need, in terms of the requirements of nature rather than other perceived needs, including the demands of pleasure—for certain foods, or clothing, or perfumes, or music, or entertainments, or sex, or wealth, or adulation and reputation. He directs them to care for the body only insofar as it may serve the soul, freeing it to pursue wisdom.

Basil finishes by expounding the usefulness of gathering together non-Christian writing having to do with virtue. Even though Christian writings are superior to these, he affirms that the many small advantages coming from such non-Christian writings can add up to a great benefit. The goal is to gather supplies for the journey of life—not only for this present life, as with Bias, but for eternity. In short, his students should always choose what is best. They should act now rather than letting the condition of their souls become so bad that they despair.

INTRODUCTION TO BASIL'S "ADDRESS TO YOUNG MEN ON THE RIGHT USE OF GREEK LITERATURE"

(1902)

The following is the introduction that Frederick Morgan Padelford included before his own version of Basil's reflections on how one may benefit from reading Greek literature. It is useful for two reasons. One, it presents a rather full biography of Basil the Great—more so, at least, than that given in The Classics Cave's introduction. Two, it offers a brief analysis of the thinking of other early Christian theologians, gnostic and otherwise, about how Christians should approach the use of non-Christian ("pagan") literature.

Though the introductory essay is offered mostly as it originally appeared, section titles have been added for ease of understanding.

The *Address to Young Men on the Right Use of Greek Literature* is not the anxious admonition of a bigoted ecclesiastic, apprehensive for the supremacy of the Sacred Writings. Rather, it is the educational theory of a cultured man, whose familiarity with classical learning and enthusiasm for it were second only to his knowledge of the Scriptures and zeal for righteousness. No student of the classics in Christian times has been more significantly placed for estimating justly the peculiar excellencies and defects of the Greek learning, and no other scholar has written with a truer perspective, and with more sanity, large-mindedness, and justice. These qualities in the address can be adequately appreciated only after the reader has become acquainted with the remarkable life of the author.

Moreover, the appreciation of the address demands not only that its pages be read in the light of the author's career, but also that the place of the essay in the development of ecclesiastical philosophy be understood.

Accordingly the following pages will attempt to give, first a survey of the life of Basil, and secondly, a review of the varieties of attitude assumed toward classical learning by those ecclesiastics who wrote prior to the time of Basil.

THE LIFE OF BASIL

St. Basil was born at Caesarea in the year 329, in a home of culture and piety. His father, who came from a family which had stood high in military and civic affairs, followed the profession of rhetoric, and was a man of wealth and of public spirit, noted for his benefactions. His grandmother, Macrina, and mother, St. Emmelia, were to him a Lois and a Eunice, and trained him in the Holy Scriptures from his infancy. Thus Basil grew up in an atmosphere of gentleness, of learning, and of Christian fervor. It is a sufficient comment upon this home life that of the ten children four became saints, St. Macrina, St. Gregory Nyssen [of Nyssa], St. Peter, and St. Basil; that three became bishops; and that St. Basil is one of thirteen upon whom the Catholic Church has conferred the title of Doctor Ecclesiae [Doctor of the Church].

When a lad, Basil was sent to Byzantium to study under Libanius, the celebrated rhetorician and sophist, then at the height of his popularity. Under this teacher the youth was trained in the felicities of Greek expression, and from him derived that love for Greek literature which led him, at the age of twenty-one, to seek the refined atmosphere of Athens, the center of learning, and the home of arts and letters. To this city resorted the most promising young men of Europe and Asia, and there they devoted themselves to the acquisition of learning with an intensity which rivaled the most flourishing days of the schools at Alexandria.

Basil was welcomed to Athens by a Cappadocian youth who had himself but just arrived, Gregory Nazianzen, and the two young men soon became fast friends. They were well adapted to each other, for the judicial exactness of Basil, and his poise — one might almost say his melancholy — were happily complemented by Gregory's intellectual brilliancy, and his liveliness of disposition. Of this friendship Gregory wrote as follows: "It was one soul which had two bodies. Eloquence, the most inspiring pursuit in the world, incited us to an equal ardor, yet without creating any jealousy whatever. We lived in each other. We knew but two walks: the first and dearest, that which led to the church and its teachers; the other, less exalted, which led to the school and its masters." [*Orat.* 43.]

A third young man who shared to some extent in this friendship was Julian, the cousin of Constantius II, then a scholarly recluse and a Christian, but soon to become emperor and an apostate.

Within a very short time, their attainments in scholarship and their remarkable ability as public speakers gave Basil and Gregory an enviable reputation, not only in Athens itself, but in every other city where learning was fostered.

After five years spent in Athens, and when he was giving every promise of an exceptional career, Basil suddenly announced his purpose to leave the city; he had been coming to feel that, with all of its learning, Athens laid emphasis upon the less essential things, that, as he expressed it, "life there was hollow blessedness." In this feeling Gregory to some extent shared, and accordingly decided to leave with his friend. When the day of departure arrived, companions and even teachers crowded around and besought them to stay, even offering violence; but although they prevailed for the time upon the more yielding Gregory, Basil was resolute, and retired to Caesarea.

For a short period he practiced law in his native city, yet, despite his brilliant *début*, his heart was not in his work, and he decided to escape from business cares and renounce the world. Accordingly, that he might determine what kind of retirement would prove most agreeable, "he traveled over much sea and land," and visited the hermits in Egypt, Syria, and Asia Minor. On his return he sought out a wild and beautiful retreat in Pontus, where, surrounded by lofty crags, a mountain stream tossing and leaping nearby, and a lovely plain spread out beneath, he erected a monastery, and established a brotherhood. This was in 358.

For four years he led here a serene and joyous life, devoted to prayer and psalmody, the study of the inspired writers, and peaceful labor. In the course of time he experienced the pleasure of a visit from his beloved friend, and years later Gregory drew a charming picture of those happy days, in which he recalled with equal pleasure the songs of praise in the rustic chapel, and the little plane-tree which he had planted with his own hands.

Occasionally Basil left his retreat to preach to the country people, or to perform deeds of mercy, as when, for example, in the course of a famine he sold his lands to provide bread for the starving inhabitants of the province. It was characteristic of the man that Jews, pagans, and Christians were treated with equal consideration.

But this attractive life was not allowed to be permanent, for Basil was summoned to Constantinople to aid the bishop of Ancyrus in his struggle with Eunomius, the new and forceful exponent of the Arian heresy. Henceforth he was never long absent from public life.

In 362 occurred an event which occasioned bitter enmity between Basil and Gregory and their college friend Julian, and threatened great injury to the cause of the church. Julian, then emperor, had invited Basil to Rome, and he was preparing to embark, when word was received that upon the standards of the army the cross of Christ had been replaced by the images of the gods. Basil correctly interpreted this as indicative of apostasy, and refused to have any further intercourse with the Emperor. Julian was greatly angered, and in retaliation decreed that the study of the classics should be denied to Christians. These were his haughty and ironical words: "For us are the eloquence and the arts of the Greeks, and the worship of the gods; for you, ignorance and rusticity, and nothing else, I fear; so, your wisdom." This was indeed bitter revenge, for the Church had found her hold upon classical learning the most effective weapon against the pagans. The indignation of Gregory gives some idea of the consternation which this decree occasioned, and of the value which he and his friend placed upon classical learning: "I forego all the rest, riches, birth, honor, authority, and all goods here below of which the charm vanishes like a dream; but I cling to oratory, nor do I regret the toil, nor the journeys by land and sea, which I have undertaken to master it."

This announcement promised to be but the beginning of a series of persecutions, but death providentially cut short the career of Julian in 363.

In the following year Basil was ordained priest by Eusebius, bishop of Caesarea, but the fame which his sermons upon the death of Julian secured for the young priest aroused the jealousy of the bishop, and Basil retired to Pontus. However, by his modest conduct he succeeded in regaining the friendship of Eusebius, and after three years was recalled to help check the Arian heresy. His learning, his ability as an orator, and his fearless but gentle conduct, all fitted him for such a task.

In 370, despite much bitter opposition, not simply on the part of strangers, but from his own uncle as well, Basil was raised to the episcopate of Caesarea. The task which devolved upon him as bishop was to cultivate a spirit of harmony and of whole-hearted service among his clergy, and, both in his own province and indirectly in the neighboring provinces, to cherish the orthodox faith as outlined in the Nicene creed.

In many respects this was the most trying period in the history of the early Church. Christians were no longer called upon to be martyrs, as had been the case a century before, but the wealth and prestige to which the Church had attained was impairing that simplicity which had made the Church of the first centuries so effective. As a result, many selfish and ambitious men were attracted to ecclesiastical service, and it was more difficult for even an unselfish man to lead a godly life. Moreover, the Church was divided into many warring factions, such as the Arians, the Semi-Arians, and the Sabellians, the Arians being especially determined and overbearing, because they had gained the support of the emperor Valens. It is to the glory of Basil that at such a time he stood for the Apostolic ideals.

Immediately upon the assumption of his new office Basil set about gaining the good will and allegiance of those of the clergy who had opposed his election. This work was progressing with reasonable expedition, when suddenly he was confronted by the emperor himself and commanded to renounce the orthodox faith. This

Basil flatly refused to do, and the cowardly Valens was awed into admiration. Henceforth Basil had nothing to fear from imperial intervention, and yet, because most of the other bishops of the East had complied with the emperor's demands, the task of supporting the true faith was rendered correspondingly more difficult. The Arians opposed him at every turn, and, what was harder to bear, the Sabellians misinterpreted his motives in trying to win back the Semi-Arians to the true faith by mildness and sympathy, and accused him of heresy. Even some of those who professed the orthodox belief, and who should have supported him in his heroic efforts to preserve the integrity of the faith, misunderstood him, and, most distressing of all, his lifelong friend Gregory accused him of attempting to turn their friendship to selfish ends. Lastly, even the Pope and the bishops of the West turned a deaf ear to his appeals for help. Is it any wonder that a body already weakened by asceticism and wasted by disease gave way in this unequal struggle?

Basil did not live to behold the triumph of the Catholic faith. He saw but the dark hour before the dawn. And yet he was victorious, victorious because he kept the rank and file of the Church in Cappadocia true to the faith of the fathers. The simple folk who hungered and thirsted after righteousness loved and followed him, attracted by his austere living, the sweetness and integrity of his character, his singleness of purpose, and his high thoughts. Small wonder that this was so, for even when oppressed with the duties of his high office and broken in body, he frequently stole away to be with these simple people, to comfort them in their afflictions, and to teach them, in sermons which delight us today equally by their Hebraic fervor and their classical form and idiom, to behold God in his handiwork. Listen as he points out to them the glory of the heavens: "There is our ancient native seat, from which the murderous demon has cast us down. If things created for time are so grand, what will be the things of eternity? If things visible are so beautiful, what will be the invisible? If the immensity of the skies surpasses the measure of human thought, what intelligence can fathom the depths of eternity? If this eye of nature, which so adorns it, this sun, which, though perishable, is yet so beautiful, so rapid in movement, so well adapted in size to the world, offers us an inexhaustible theme for contemplation, what will be the beauty of the sun of divine righteousness?"

Or again: "If the ocean is beautiful and worthy of praise to God, how much more beautiful is the conduct of this Christian assembly, where the voices of men, women, and children, blended and sonorous like the waves that break upon the beach, rise amidst our prayers to the very presence of God!"

Basil's death occurred on January 1st, 279, when he was but fifty years of age. Like many another valiant soldier of the Cross, he died with these words upon his lips: "Into thy hands I commend my spirit." The scene at his funeral was an impressive one. The entire province was given over to grief, and pagans and Jews united with Christians in their lamentations. As the funeral procession advanced, many perished in their desire to approach the coffin, but they were accounted happy to die on such a day, and the people called them the funeral victims.

So lived and died this scholar and man of God.

EARLY CHRISTIAN RESPONSES TO GREEK LEARNING

Let us now turn from the life of St. Basil to a brief consideration of the *Address to Young Men* in relation to the attitude assumed by earlier ecclesiastics toward Greek learning.

If we condense the thought of the essay into the fewest words, the result is something as follows: While classical philosophy, oratory, and poetry even at their best do not reveal the truth with absolute accuracy, they yet reflect it as in a mirror; the truth may be seen face to face only in the Scriptures, yet it is possible in the pagan writings to trace, as it were, its silhouette. Accordingly, for those who are not yet prepared for the strong meat of the Scriptures, the study of Greek literature is a valuable preparatory course.

This is virtually the attitude taken toward classical learning by several of the early Church writers, and, therefore a survey of so much of the ecclesiastical philosophy as concerns Greek poetry and philosophy will help to establish the antecedents of Basil's essay.

It was inevitable that, when Christianity came in contact with the speculative genius of the Greeks and the Oriental pantheistic naturalism, there should be an effort to advance from Christian faith to Christian knowledge, and to discover a philosophic basis for the teachings of the Holy Scriptures. This first effort was made by the so-called Gnostics, who exerted their greatest influence in the middle of the second century. The Hellenic Gnostics attempted to employ the writings of the Greek philosophers to explain the Scriptures, but the many perplexing questions which they strove to answer soon led them as far away from the doctrines of Plato as from those of Paul. Beginning with the attempt to discover the allegorical significance of the Scriptures, Gnosticism ended in mere chimerical speculation, in mysticism, mythology, and theosophy. It exerted little permanent influence, and by the time of Basil was no longer a force in religious controversy.

Contemporaneously with the flourishing of Gnosticism, however, wrote Justin Martyr, who influenced very much the ecclesiastical writers of the East during the third and fourth centuries. As a young man Justin made a thorough study of the Greek philosophy, being especially attracted to the writings of Plato and of the Stoics, but as he grew older his admiration for the fortitude of the Christians, and for their sublime faith—an admiration which was intensified by his growing distrust in the sovereignty of human reason—led him to embrace Christianity. Henceforth he was the champion of the new religion. This, however, was not at the expense of Greek philosophy, for his breadth of view enabled him to recognize the worth both of the profane and of the Sacred Writings.

Justin bases his philosophy upon the Logos of John's Gospel. Wherever truth is found, it is an expression of the divine Logos; Plato, Homer, Pythagoras, and Solon received partial revelations of it, and indeed it reveals itself somewhat to every man, though the one perfect and complete revelation is Christ, who is the Logos incarnate.

For our present purpose we need observe in detail only that phase of Justin's philosophy which is concerned with classical literature. Greek philosophy and poetry are to be esteemed highly, because, to an unusual degree, they express the divine revelation. Not only did such men as Homer and Plato experience revelations of the truth, but they were also familiar with the teachings of Moses, and indeed with all of the Old Testament. Such doctrines in Plato as eternal punishment, the immortality of the soul, and the freedom of the will, were borrowed from the early Jewish books.

Of the other four prominent apologists of the second century, Tatian, Hernias, and Theophilus condemn and ridicule Greek philosophy, and Athenagoras assumes an attitude similar to that of Justin. Tatian, who was an Assyrian, abused all things Greek with barbaric severity, Hermas wrote an *Abuse of the Pagan Philosophers*, and Theophilus called the doctrines of the Greek philosophers foolishness. Athenagoras, on the other hand, esteemed the Greek philosophers, and quoted them in support of the unity of God, a truth which he believed the Spirit had revealed to them despite the prevailing polytheism of their country.

The closing years of the second century and the first half of the third were engrossed in the controversy which the Gnostics had aroused. Anti-Gnosticism found its most spirited champion in Tertullian, the foremost Latin ecclesiastical writer of the early centuries. Tertullian believed that Christianity alone possessed the truth, that philosophy was the source of all heresies, and that Plato and other Greek philosophers, though they had stolen certain isolated truths from Moses, which they arrogated to themselves, were exponents of falsehood. So extreme was his antipathy to philosophy that he eventually declared: *Credo quid absurdum est* [I believe because it is absurd].

On the other hand Clement of Alexandria and his pupil, Origen, the founder of the school to which Basil, Gregory of Nyssa, and Gregory Nazianzen adhered, endeavored to separate the true from the false in Gnosticism. Both of them laid much stress upon the value of Greek philosophy.

Ueberweg gives the following comprehensive digest of Clement's views concerning the relation of the pagan writings to the Scriptures: "Clement adopts the view of Justin, that to Christianity, as the whole truth, the conceptions of ante-Christian times are opposed, not as mere errors, but as partial truths. The divine Logos, which is everywhere poured out, like the light of the sun (*Stromata* v. 3), enlightened the souls of men from the beginning. It instructed the Jews through Moses and the prophets (*Paedagogus* i. 7). Among the Greeks, on the contrary, it called forth wise men, and gave them, through the mediation of the lower angels, whom the Logos had appointed to be shepherds of the nations (*Strom.* vii. 2), philosophy as a guide to righteousness (*Strom.* i. 5; vi. 5). Like Justin, Clement maintains that the philosophers took much of their doctrine secretly from the Orientals, and, in particular, from the religious books of the Jews, which doctrine they then, from desire of renown, falsely proclaimed as the result of their own independent investigations, besides falsifying and corrupting it *(Strom.* i. i. 17; *Paed.* ii. i). Yet some things pertaining to true doctrine were really discovered by the Greek philosophers, by the aid of the seed of the divine Logos implanted in them *(Cohortatio* vi. 59). Plato was the best of the Greek philosophers (*Paed.* iii. 11; *Strom.* v. 8). The Christian must choose out that which is true in the writings of the different philosophers, *i.e.,* whatever agrees with Christianity *(Strom.* i. 7; vi. 17). We need the aid of philosophy in order to advance from faith to knowledge. The Gnostic is to him who merely believes without knowing as the grown-up man to the child; having outgrown the fear of the Old Testament, he has arrived at a higher stage of the divine plan of man's education. Whoever will attain to Gnosis without philosophy, dialectic, and the study of nature, is like him who expects to gather grapes without cultivating the grapevine *(Strom.* i. 9). But the criterion of true science must always be the harmony of the latter with faith (*Strom.* ii. 4)."

Of Origen, who was the last ecclesiastical philosopher of influence in the Eastern church prior to the fourth century, it is enough to say that he assumed the same attitude toward the Greek writers as did his master.

One who has read Basil's essay will readily appreciate the similarity between the views of Basil and those of Justin, Athenagoras, Clement, and Origen. The chapters in the essay might almost be arranged as expositions of the various elements in the above digest from Clement's writings. There is the same belief in the partial inspiration of the Greek poets and philosophers, the same advocacy of the study of Hellenic literature as an introduction to the study of Christianity, the common credence in the indebtedness of Plato and other philosophers to Moses and the Prophets, and the like insistence upon life as a growth, and upon knowledge as the complement of faith.

To summarize this brief review: For at least two centuries before Basil wrote his *Address to Young Men on the Right Use of Greek Literature* [that is, *How to Benefit from Reading Greek Literature*] efforts had been made to determine the true relation between Greek learning and Christianity. Some writers bitterly opposed Hellenic philosophy and poetry, others recognized that it contained a partial revelation of the truth. To the latter view Justin and his followers inclined, and among these followers one of the most pronounced is Basil.

THE VALUE OF GREEK LITERATURE
AMONG OTHER EARLY CHURCH FATHERS
Justin Martyr and Clement of Alexandria*

T HE EARLY CHURCH Fathers had mixed views regarding the classics, whether poetry or prose, mythology, drama, philosophy, or otherwise. The following selections present two of the more positive views regarding "outside" or "pagan" (non-Christian) literature that would have influenced Basil the Great. Brief explanations of each are given in italics.

For Justin Martyr (second century), philosophy is "the greatest possession" that leads human beings to God.

Justin Martyr Philosophy is, in fact, the greatest possession, and most honorable before God, to whom it leads us and alone commends us. And these are truly holy men who have bestowed attention on philosophy. What philosophy is, however, and the reason why it has been sent down to men, have escaped the observation of most—for there would be neither Platonists, nor Stoics, nor Peripatetics, nor Theoretics (Skeptics), nor Pythagoreans, since this knowledge is one.[1]

With Clement of Alexandria (second and early third century), we see a far more positive assessment of outside literature. In short, Clement—the open-minded theologian and earnest catechist of Alexandria—values Greek and Latin literature for the truth it conveys. Philosophy, he declares, is something good. And nothing truly evil (such as demons) can produce anything good, he argues. Rather than being harmful, philosophy "is the clear image of truth, a divine gift to the Greeks." In the past, philosophy was for the Greeks the means by which they were righteous; it was a "preparatory training" for the coming of Christ, he reasons, "just as the law was for the Hebrews."

Clement of Alexandria Our book will not shrink from making use of what is best in philosophy and other preparatory instruction. . . . And, in truth, to speak briefly, among many small pearls there is the one. And in a great take of fish there is the beauty-fish. And by time and toil truth will gleam forth if a good helper is at hand. For most benefits are supplied from God through men.

All of us who make use of our eyes see what is presented before them. Even so, some look at objects for one reason, others for another. For instance, the cook and the shepherd do not survey the sheep in a similar manner. The one examines it to see if it is fat. The other watches to see if it is of good breed. Let a man milk the sheep's milk if he needs sustenance. Let him shear the wool if he needs clothing. And in this way let me produce the fruit of the Greek erudition. . . .

For, like farmers who irrigate the land beforehand, so we also water with the liquid stream of Greek learning what in it is earthy, so that it may receive the spiritual seed cast into it and may be capable of easily nourishing it.

The *Stromata* [Clement's book] will contain the truth mixed up in the teachings of philosophy, or rather covered over and hidden, as the edible part of the nut in the shell. For, in my opinion, it is fitting that the seeds of truth be kept for the cultivator of faith, and no others.

I am not unaware of what is babbled by some, who in their ignorance are frightened at every noise and say that we should occupy ourselves with what is most necessary and that which contains the faith. And that we should pass over what is beyond and superfluous, that which wears us out and pointlessly detains us without leading us to the great end.

Others think that philosophy was introduced into life by an evil influence for the ruin of men, by an evil inventor. But I will show, throughout the whole of these *Stromata*, that evil has an evil nature and can never be the producer of anything that is good. This indicates that philosophy is in a sense a work of divine providence. . . .

Philosophy does not ruin life by being the originator of false practices and base deeds—though some have slandered it in this way, even though it is the clear image of truth, a divine gift to the Greeks. Nor does philosophy drag us away from the faith, as if we were bewitched by some deceptive art. Rather, so to speak, by the use of an ampler circuit, it achieves a common exercise demonstrative of the faith. Furthermore, the juxtaposition of doctrines, by comparison, preserves the truth from which follows knowledge. . . .

Accordingly, before the advent of the Lord, philosophy was necessary to the Greeks for righteousness. And now it becomes conducive to piety, being a kind of preparatory training to those who come to faith through demonstration. For your foot, it is said, will not stumble if you refer what is good—whether belonging to the Greeks or to us—to providence. For God is the cause of all good things—of some primarily, as with the Old and the New Testament, and of others by consequence, as with philosophy. It is possible, too, that philosophy was given to the Greeks directly and primarily, until the Lord called the Greeks. For philosophy was a schoolmaster to bring the Hellenic [Greek] mind to Christ, just as the law was for the Hebrews. Philosophy, therefore, was a preparation, paving the way for him who is perfected in Christ. . . .

And philosophy—I do not mean the Stoic, or the Platonic, or the Epicurean, or the Aristotelian, but whatever has been well said by each of those schools that teach righteousness along with a knowledge pervaded by piety—this eclectic whole I call philosophy. . . .

These are the times of the oldest wise men and philosophers among the Greeks. And that most of them were barbarians by extraction and were trained among [non-Greek or Roman] barbarians, what need is there to say? Pythagoras is shown to have been either a Tuscan or a Tyrian. And Antisthenes was a Phrygian. And Orpheus was an Odrysian or a Thracian. The majority also show Homer to have been an Egyptian. Thales was a Phoenician by birth, and was said to have consorted with the prophets of the Egyptians.[2] So did Pythagoras associate with the same persons by whom he was circumcised. He did this so that he could enter the innermost sanctuary and learn the mystic philosophy from the Egyptians. Moreover, he conversed with the chief of the Chaldeans and the Magi. And he gave a hint of the Church—now so-called—in the common hall that he maintained. And Plato does not deny that he procured all that is most excellent in philosophy from the barbarians. . . .

Later on, we will address the plagiarizing of the Greek philosophers—how they took their teachings from the Hebrews. But first, as due order demands, we must now speak of the time of Moses, by which the philosophy of the Hebrews will be demonstrated beyond all contradiction to be the most ancient of all wisdom. . . .

As for the Greeks, Homer and Hesiod are much more recent than the Trojan War. And after them the lawgivers among the Greeks are far more recent, Lycurgus and Solon, and the seven wise men, and Pherecydes of Syros, and Pythagoras the Great, who lived later, about the Olympiads, as we have shown. We have also demonstrated Moses to be more ancient, not only than those called poets and wise men among the Greeks, but older than most of their gods.[3]

Clement of Alexandria The same God that furnished both the covenants was the one who gave to the Greeks their philosophy by which the Almighty is glorified among the Greeks. . . .

So then, from the Hellenic training, and also from that of the law, are gathered into the one kind of saved people those who accept faith. . . . But as the proclamation [of the Gospel] has come now at the right time, so also at the right time were the Law and the Prophets given to the barbarians and philosophy to the Greeks to prepare their ears for the Gospel. . . . And in general terms, we will not err in alleging that all things necessary and profitable for life came to us from God, and that, in particular, philosophy was given to the Greeks as a covenant peculiar to them—being, as it is, a stepping-stone to the philosophy that is according to Christ.[4]

Clement of Alexandria The multitude are frightened by Greek philosophy as children are at masks, being afraid that it will lead them astray. . . . *Nevertheless,* the mature Christian takes advantage of *other* branches of learning as auxiliary preparatory exercises in order to accurately communicate the truth as far as attainable and with as little distraction as possible. He does so for defense against reasonings that plot for the extinction of the truth. He will not then be deficient in what contributes to proficiency in the curriculum of studies and the Hellenic philosophy.[5]

Clement of Alexandria How absurd, then, is it, to those who attribute disorder and wickedness to the devil, to make him the bestower of philosophy, a virtuous thing! For in this way he is all but made more benevolent to the Greeks, relative to making men good, in comparison with the divine providence and mind. . . . Philosophy is not, then, the product of vice since it makes men virtuous. It follows, then, that it is the work of God, whose activity it is solely to do good. And all things given by God are given and received well.[6]

Clement discusses how Greek literature may be used for the benefit of those Greek catechumens who are learning about Christianity for the first time.

Clement of Alexandria He who collects what is useful from Hellenic studies for the advantage of the catechumens, and particularly when they are Greeks, . . . must not abstain from erudition, like irrational animals. Rather, he must collect as many aids as possible for his student hearers. Even so, he must by no means linger over these studies, except solely for the advantage that comes from them—so that, on grasping and obtaining this, he may be able to depart for home to the true philosophy [of Christ], which is a strong cable for the soul, providing security from everything.[7]

Clement believed that even if a person has studied Greek philosophy, he or she must nevertheless turn to Christ and the Christian philosophy.

Clement of Alexandria The Lord says in explanation, I am the door of the sheep. Men must then be saved by learning the truth through Christ, even if they attain philosophy. For now that is clearly shown which was not made known to other ages, which is now revealed to the sons of men. For there was always a natural manifestation of the one almighty God, among all right-thinking men.[8]

Finally, Clement suggests that a mature Christian may peruse Greek philosophy in his spare time, consuming it not as the main meal that provides true sustenance, but for dessert, as it were.

Clement of Alexandria A mature Christian always occupies himself with the things of highest importance. But if at any time he has leisure and time for relaxation from what is of primary importance, he applies himself to Hellenic philosophy in preference to other recreation, feasting on it as a kind of dessert at supper.[9]

*To read more about how the early Church Fathers (and others through history) approached and valued the classics, whether Greek or Latin, see The Classics Cave's *The Value of the Classics: What the Ancient Greeks, Romans, and Others Have Thought and Said about the Classics.*

NOTES

[1] Justin Martyr, *Dialogue with Trypho* 2.

[2] One should take Clement's general point here rather than (necessarily) his identification of origins for each of these men.

[3] Clement of Alexandria, *Stromata* 1.1-2; 5; 7; 15; 21.

[4] Ibid., 6.5, 6, 8.

[5] Ibid., 6.10. To avoid confusion, we have replaced Clement's "Gnostic" (*gnōstikos*) with "mature Christian." By "Gnostic," Clement did not mean a Gnostic Christian in the sense that Basilides and Valentinian (both criticized by Clement) were Gnostics; rather, he simply meant a Christian mature in knowledge, virtue, and the like. For more on Clement's *gnōstikos*, see ibid 6.9-10; 7.1, 3, 7-8, 11-14.

[6] Ibid., 6.37.

[7] Ibid., 6.11.

[8] Ibid., 5.13.

[9] Ibid., 6.38. Regarding "mature Christian," see the note for 6.10.

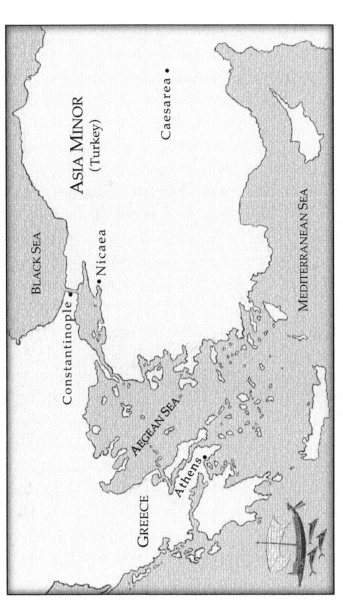

Greece and Asia Minor

Born in Caesarea, Basil was educated in Constantinople and Athens before returning to his homeland in what is today Turkey.

GLOSSARY

OF ENGLISH WORDS AND GREEK EQUIVALENTS
THAT APPEAR IN BASIL'S ADDRESS

Action; an act, a doing; a deed: *praxis* (πρᾶξις).

Adultery; adulterous affair: *moicheia* (μοιχεία).

Advantage, gain, profit: *kerdos* (κέρδος).

To advise, counsel: *sumbouleuō* (συμβουλεύω).

Affinity; relationship, friendliness, connection: *oikeiotēs* (οἰκειότης).

Beauty: *kallos* or *kalos* (κάλλος or καλός).

Bee: *melissa* (μέλισσα). **Honey**: *meli* (μέλι).

Benefit, profit; help: *ōpheleia* (ὠφέλεια). **Advantage**: *ophelos* (ὄφελος).

Body: *sōma* (σῶμα).

Captain, steersman, pilot: *kubernētēs* (κυβερνήτης).

Contest; a struggle, trial; battle: *agōn* (ἀγών).

Desire; love: *erōs* (ἔρως). **Longing**, yearning, desire: *epithumia* (ἐπιθυμία).

Dream: *onar* (ὄναρ).

Education, training: *paideia* (παιδεία).

Example, model, pattern: *paradeigma* (παράδειγμα).

Famous, notable, held in account: *ellogimos* (ἐλλόγιμος).

Flower, bloom: *anthos* (ἄνθος).

Goal, end, target: *telos* (τέλος).

God: *theos* (θεός). **Gods**: *theoi* (θεοί).

Good: *agathos* (ἀγαθός).

Goodwill, kindness, favor: *eunoia* (εὔνοια).

Happiness, prosperity: *eudaimonia* (εὐδαιμονία). **Happy**, prosperous: *eudaimōn* (εὐδαίμων).

Harmful: *blaberos* (βλαβερός).

Honor, honors: *timē* (τιμή). **To scorn**, dishonor: *atimazō* (ἀτιμάζω).

Hope: *elpis* (ἐλπίς).

Imitation: *mimēsis* (μίμησις).

Light: *phaos* (φάος).

Mind: *nous* (νοῦς).

Moderation, temperance, self-control: *sōphrosunē* (σωφροσύνη).

Noble, good: *esthlos* (ἐσθλός).

Outside (writers, writings—implied; thus, "pagan"): *exō* (ἔξω).
Passions, feelings: *pathos* (πάθος).
Philosopher, lover of wisdom: *philosophos* (φιλόσοφος).
Plasticity, softness: *hapalotēs* (ἁπαλότης).
Pleasure, delight, enjoyment: *hēdonē* (ἡδονή).
Poet, maker: *poiētēs* (ποιητής).
Possession(s); valuable(s), good(s): *chrēma* (χρῆμα).
Prayer, prayers: *euchē* (εὐχή).
Preliminary training; to train beforehand: *progumnazō* (προγυμνάζω).
Prison: *desmōtērion* (δεσμωτήριον).
Profitable, advantageous, useful: *lusitelēs* (λυσιτελής).
Prose writer: *sungrapheus* (συγγραφεύς).
Punishment, correction: *kolasis* (κόλασις).
In reality; true, what is true: *alēthēs* (ἀληθής). **Truth**: *alētheia* (ἀλήθεια).
Rose garden; bed of roses: *rhodōnia* (ῥοδωνιά).
Sacred writings; sacred words: *hieroi logoi* (ἱεροί λόγοι).
Sensation; sense-perception; one of the senses: *aisthēsis* (αἴσθησις).
Shadow, shadows: *skia* (σκιά).
Soul: *psuchē* or *psychē* (ψυχή).
Sun: *hēlios* (ἥλιος).
Sweat: *hidrōs* (ἱδρώς).
System of education: *paideusis* (παίδευσις). Related to the rearing of a
    child: *pais* (παῖς); and to **education**, training: *paideia* (παιδεία).
To **teach**, instruct: *didaskō* (διδάσκω).
Toil, hard work; suffering: *ponos* (πόνος).
Traveling supplies: *ephodion* (ἐφόδιον).
Useful, serviceable, good for use, good: *chrēsimos* (χρήσιμος). **Useless**,
    unprofitable: *achreios* (ἀχρεῖος).
Valuable, valued: *timios* (τίμιος).
Vice; badness, wickedness: *kakia* (κακία). Also: *ponēria* (πονηρία).
Vicissitude, change: *metabolē* (μεταβολή).
Virtue; goodness, excellence: *aretē* (ἀρετή).
Way, path, road: *hodos* (ὁδός).
Wealth, riches: *ploutos* (πλοῦτος).
Wisdom: *sophia* (σοφία). **Philosophy**; love of wisdom: *philosophia*
    (φιλοσοφία).

SOURCES AND FURTHER READING

This Classics Cave rendition of Basil's address *On How to Benefit from Reading Greek Literature* was made using the Greek text found in Roy J. Deferrari (1926; 1934), with an eye on F. Boulenger's Greek text (1935) found in N.G. Wilson.

SUGGESTIONS FOR FURTHER READING

Chadwick, Henry. *Early Christian Thought and the Classical Tradition: Studies in Justin, Clement, and Origen.* Oxford: The Clarendon Press, 1966.

Cribiore, Rafaella. *Gymnastics of the Mind: Greek Education in Hellenistic and Roman Egypt.* Princeton: Princeton University Press, 2001.

Deferrari, Roy J. Basil: *Letters 249-368; On Greek Literature.* Vol. 3 of *Basil: Letters.* Cambridge: Harvard University Press, 1934.

Dodd, E.R. *Pagan and Christian in an Age of Anxiety.* Cambridge: Cambridge University Press, 1965.

Downey, Glanville. "Education in the Christian Roman Empire: Christian Theories under Constantine and His Successors." *Speculum* 32 (1957): 48-61.

Fortin, Ernest L. "Christianity and Hellenism in Basil the Great's Address *Ad Adulescentes.*" In *Neoplatonism and Early Christian Thought,* edited by Blumenthal and Markus, 189-203. London: Variorum, 1981.

Gregg, Robert Clark. *Consolation Philosophy: Greek and Christian Paideia in Basil and the Two Gregories.* Patristic Monograph Series 3. Cambridge: Philadelphia Patristic Foundation, 1975.

Hildebrand, Stephen M. *Basil of Caesarea.* Grand Rapids: Baker Academic, 2014.

Jaeger, Werner. *Early Christianity and Greek Paideia.* Cambridge: Harvard University Press, 1961.

Jones, Marvin. *Basil of Caesarea: His Life and Impact.* Fearn: Christian Focus Publications, 2014.

O'Meara, Dominic J. *Neoplatonism and Christian Thought*. Albany: State University of New York Press, 1982.

Padelford, Frederick Morgan. *Essays on the Study and Use of Poetry by Plutarch and Basil the Great*. New York: Henry Hold and Company, 1902.

Rousseau, Philip. *Basil of Caesarea*. Berkeley: University of California Press, 1994.

Schoedel, William R., and Robert L. Wilken, eds. *Early Christian Literature and the Classical Intellectual Tradition: In Honorem Robert M. Grant*. Théologie historique 54. Paris: Beauchesne, 1979.

Shear, Theodore Leslie. *The Influence of Plato on St. Basil*. Baltimore: J.H. Furst, 1906.

The Classics Cave. *The Value of the Classics: What the Ancient Greeks, Romans, and Others through History Have Thought and Said about the Classics*. Sugar Land: The Classics Cave, 2021.

Wayman, Benjamin. D. "Julian against Christian Educators: Julian and Basil on a Proper Education." *Christian Scholar's Review* 45, no. 3 (2016): 249-267.

Wilson, N.G. ed. *Saint Basil on Greek Literature*. London: Gerald Duckworth & Co., 1975.

————. *Scholars of Byzantium*. Revised edition. London: Gerald Duckworth & Co., 1996.

Young, Frances M. *Biblical Exegesis and the Formation of Christian Culture*. New York: Cambridge University Press, 1997.

————. "The Rhetorical Schools and Their Influence on Patristic Exegesis." In *The Making of Orthodoxy: Essays in Honour of Henry Chadwick*, edited by Rowan Williams, 182-99. New York: Cambridge University Press, 1989.

THE CLASSICS CAVE CATALOGUE

— OF —

CAVE OFFERINGS, BOOKS & GOODS

www.theclassicscave.com

Read more from The Classics Cave!
The following is some
of what The Classics Cave is working on.
These offerings, books, and goods will be fully available
by the late summer of 2021.

■　■　■

CAVE OFFERINGS

Supported by our sponsors and the members of the Adopt an Ancient Author Society,
the following Cave Offerings are free. Experience them at www.theclassicscave.com.

CAVE FIRST WORDS (FW)

Sign up for each member of the Cave First Words family at
www.theclassicscave.com (available summer 2021)

FW *Bonfire*—offers wide-ranging topical and thematic explorations. Find out what the Greeks thought and said about literature, liberty, happiness, war, virtue, desire, beauty, natural law, pleasure, and more.

FW *Slow Burn*—presents longer selections of Greek literature and philosophy for contemplation and discussion. Keep your mind sharp and heart courageous with what the Greeks felt, thought, said, and did.

FW *Fireside Chat*—delivers in-depth interviews. Come near to the fire and listen to what your favorite Greek poet, historian, or philosopher has to say about him or herself and life.

FW *Kindle*—explores the intersection of the ancient and modern worlds. Discover how antiquity and the classics have influenced our world today.

FW *Reflection*—presents thought-provoking passages, soulful reflections, life-building workbook exercises, and challenging journal prompts. Do a deep dive within with the help of the ancient Greeks.

FW *Lighthouse* (or Ask the Ancients)—offers the counsel of the ancient Greeks (and Romans) with the backing of modern psychology, counseling, and practice. What's your question? For what would you like advice? Just ask the ancients. Navigate life with FW *Lighthouse*.

FW *Spark*—promises captivating ancient conversation starters along with kindling questions. You want something to talk about? Light up your conversation with a FW *Spark*.

FW *Daily Light*—delivers a saying, anecdote, or other brief passage from the ancient Greeks (or Romans) each day. Listen to what antiquity has to say. For wisdom. For inspiration. For fun.

THE ANCIENT AUTHORS CAVE

Cast of Significant Greeks & Their Works • Author Interviews • Notes • Literature Summaries • Basic Facts • Big Themes & Ideas • Illustrations • Schools of Philosophy • Plans of Life • Suggestions for Further Reading • Images for Coloring • Adopt an Ancient Author Society • And More!

THE EDUCATORS CAVE

Plans • Discussion Questions • Essay Prompts • Group Projects • Topical & Thematic Expositions • Notes • Literature Summaries • Maps • Charts • Glossaries • Images for Coloring • And More!

CAVE BROCHURES & PAMPHLETS

The Value of the Classics • Introduction to The Classics Cave • Adopt an Ancient Author Society • Cave First Words • And More!

CAVE SERIES & BOOKS

Available in both paperback and e-copy at www.theclassicscave.com,
online retailers, and in stores.*

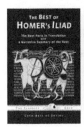    

CAVE BEST OF SERIES
The best of the classics for today

The Best of Homer's *Iliad*
The Best of Homer's *Odyssey*
The Best of Homer's *Iliad* and *Odyssey* (combined in one volume)
The Best of Hesiod's *Theogony & Works and Days*
The Best of Plato's *Republic**
The Best of Plato's *Symposium**
The Best of Plato's Literature of Ascent*
The Best of Plato*
The Best of Aristotle's *Nicomachean Ethics**
The Best of Aristotle*
The Best of the Cynics
The Best of Early Stoicism
The Best of Epicurus
The Best of the Hellenistic Philosophers*
The Best of Epictetus' *Handbook**
The Best of Basil the Great on Reading Literature and Education
The Best of Ancient Greek Literature

CAVE BONFIRE SERIES
The best of the ancient Greeks for today

Happiness: What the Ancient Greeks Thought and Said
about Happiness

CAVE BONFIRE SERIES
continued

Aretē (Excellence or Virtue): What the Ancient Greeks
Thought and Said about *Aretē*
The Value of the Classics: What the Ancient Greeks, Romans, and
Others through History Have Thought and
Said about the Classics

CAVE WISDOM & WAY SERIES: POCKET EDITION
Classical wisdom and pathways for today

The Wisdom & Way of Homer
The Wisdom & Way of Hesiod
The Wisdom & Way of Plato*
The Wisdom & Way of Aristotle*
The Wisdom & Way of the Cynics
The Wisdom & Way of the Early Stoics
The Wisdom & Way of Epicurus
The Wisdom & Way of Basil the Great
The Wisdom & Way of the Hellenistic Philosophers*
The Wisdom & Way of Ancient Greek Happiness*
The Wisdom & Way of Ancient Greek Virtue (*Aretē*)*

CAVE CLASSICS SERIES
The classics for today

Hesiod: *Theogony & Works and Days**
The Cynics: Cynic Philosophy for Desiring, Enduring & Living Well
Epicurus: How to Think Wisely, Live Well & Be Happy
Early Stoicism: Stoic Philosophy for Living Well & Happiness
Epictetus: *Handbook**
Basil the Great: *How to Benefit from Reading Greek Literature*

CAVE WORKBOOK & JOURNAL SERIES
Classics-inspired contemplation and growth for today

Know Yourself Workbook & Journal
Plato Workbook & Journal*
Aristotle Workbook & Journal*
The Cynics Workbook & Journal
The Early Stoics Workbook & Journal
Epicurus Workbook & Journal
Basil the Great Workbook & Journal
The Hellenistic Philosophers Workbook & Journal*

CAVE SPARKS SERIES
Classics-inspired conversation starters for today

Homer & Hesiod: Greek Epic Poetry Cave Sparks*
Plato Cave Sparks*
Aristotle Cave Sparks*
The Cynics Cave Sparks
The Early Stoics Cave Sparks
Epicurus Cave Sparks
Basil the Great Cave Sparks
The Hellenistic Philosophers Cave Sparks*

CAVE OPEN JOURNALS
Classics-inspired space for contemplation today

The Ancient Greeks Open Journal*
Plato Open Journal*
Aristotle Open Journal*
The Cynics Open Journal
The Early Stoics Open Journal
Epicurus Open Journal
The Hellenistic Philosophers Open Journal*

CAVE COLORING BOOK SERIES
Classics-based images for coloring

The Trojan War: A Coloring Book
The Adventures of Odysseus: A Coloring Book

CAVE GOODS

WEARABLES
with "The Classics Cave" & Logo

T-Shirt: The Classics Cave
Polo Shirt: The Classics Cave*
Baseball Cap: The Classics Cave

OTHER CAVE GOODS

Mug: The Classics Cave
Refrigerator Magnet: The Classics Cave
Bumper Sticker: The Classics Cave
Poster: Hesiod's Cosmos*
Poster: *Aretē* (Virtue or Excellence):
The Primary & Secondary Virtues*
Poster: The Classics Cave
(illustrated with Cave Books and Cave Series)*
Stationary Cards: Various (illustrated)*

* Look for these projected titles and offerings in the summer of 2021 and onward.
Offerings without an asterisk will appear during the first half of 2021.

Made in the USA
Las Vegas, NV
11 August 2022